DEVELOPING AND BUILDING
THE MIND AND HEART OF
CHRIST JESUS

DEVELOPING AND BUILDING THE MIND AND HEART OF
CHRIST JESUS

(WITHIN YOU)

A Living Devotion

DR. DAVID GARTY

To order additional copies of this book, contact:
Xlibris
844-714-8691
www.Xlibris.com
Orders@Xlibris.com
828131

Contents

Preface

It is the heart's longing of every parent to see their children grow up and reach a level of maturity that causes them to be productive as they contribute to society. Parents will do almost anything to help their children to become successful at whatever event they would like to become a part of. Many parents will even find ways to advance the skill level of their children by placing them or taking them to special programs or schools that help and teach a high level of technique and technology in the desired areas of expertise they are seeking to grow and mature in. It's truly amazing to witness the belief that many parents have and display in their children's abilities for being successful. But there is one thing that is even more interesting, and that is how much time and money parents are willing to spend on the success of their children's development.

Just a few weeks ago, I was sitting in a barbershop looking at a sport magazine waiting to get my hair cut, reading an article on some of the major colleges' quarterbacks who at the starting age of eleven years old were being placed under the care of personal professional trainers, who mentored them until they were able to sign a letter of intent with a major college.

The developing of our children's skills and abilities should be a heartfelt desire by all of us as parents. But as a believer and follower of Jesus Christ, I find myself with a longing to see the growth and maturity of my fellow brothers and sisters in their personal relationship with Jesus Christ. It is here that I ask myself how much time and how much of my life am I willing to spend to encourage the growth and maturity of my fellow brothers and sisters in Jesus Christ. This is the reason for the writing of this book, *Developing and Building the Mind and Heart of Christ Jesus.*

What will it take for each and every believer to develop the mind and heart of Christ Jesus? It is my hope that through the writing of this book I can create a process that we can follow and practice for the development of the mind and heart of Christ Jesus. The developing of our minds and hearts is the core issue here for every true believer in Jesus Christ. Our minds and hearts must be involved together with the empowerment of the Holy Spirit for true growth and maturity as the children of God. It is a true fact that our eternal destiny will be decided by the issues settled on from our minds and hearts.

Again, it's my longing to see every true follower of Jesus Christ grow and mature into the full potential of who they are in Him, their real life. Most of the Christian life is taught from the perspective of doing, which often leads to a work or performance mentality. This mindset creates a continual struggling that often leads to up-and-down experiences.

The scriptures teach that our relationship with Christ Jesus is not about our doing something but about being the true sons and daughters of God we are in Christ Jesus. What is truly needed in the life of each and every believer is an intentional internal focused faith that learns to truly visualize the spiritual reality of who they are from their position and identity in Christ Jesus. Just listen to these words of truth and life: "Your old life is dead. Your new life, which is your real life—even though invisible to spectators—is with Christ in God. He is your life. When Christ (your real life, remember) shows up again on this earth, you'll show up, too—the real you, the glorious you. Meanwhile, be content with obscurity, like Christ" (Colossians 3:3–4 MSG). We are truly called and purposed to let Christ Jesus live in our place, who has become our real life.

This book is written to be a devotional and written with thoughts and eternal life points that will help create intentional internal focused faith, creating a mindset that will help create the thoughts, attitudes, words, and actions that establish one's being.

An eternal life point is a spiritual truth that exists in God the Father and must be seen through the eyes of the Holy Spirit. As this spiritual truth begins to manifest itself within the mind and heart of the believer, it will find itself becoming a physical reality in the life of the believer. This brings Heaven's realities to earth through the lived lives of each believer. Being led and transformed by the creative work of the Holy Spirit should be a key heart issue for every believer. Revelation is not released because one simply wants insight into an issue or matter that they want to understand for their own glorification and benefit. Revelation is a transforming truth that has heavenly potential to establish Heaven's presence on earth that will have life-changing effects on all of humanity.

ETERNAL LIFE POINT: A believer's highest priority is to live for the will of God and for the sake of Jesus Christ in behalf of others. Obedience is your declaration to receiving the Holy Spirit by your submission to the leading of the Spirit. (You are the living gospel!) (Luke 9:23–24) your obedience to the Word of God is the truest form that you have experienced God's unconditional love.

ETERNAL LIFE POINT: Following the lead of the Holy Spirit is having the ability to see the invisible while doing the impossible by the creative empowerment of the Holy Spirit.

ETERNAL LIFE POINT: Being led by the Holy Spirit is a part of the transforming work of the Spirit to create and bring every believer into the image of Christ Jesus while manifesting heavenly realities in and through the life of the believer to the world around them.

ETERNAL LIFE POINT: Being creates a natural flow of being God's good work in Christ Jesus.

Room has been created for you to reflect and write your discovery of your position and identity throughout this book. My prayer for you is that you will grow and mature in your position of being His son and daughter through intentional internal focused faith.

This writing is not created to be a daily devotional but is one that may take a week or more to truly complete. It's truly about your maturity and growth in Jesus Christ.

Made Alive in Christ

And you were dead in your trespasses and sins, in which you formerly walked according to the course of this world, according to the prince of the power of the air, of the spirit that is now working in the sons of disobedience. Among them we too all formerly lived in the lusts of our flesh, indulging the desires of the flesh and of the mind, and were by nature children of wrath, even as the rest. But God, being rich in mercy, because of His great love with which He loved us, even when we were dead in our transgressions, made us alive together with Christ (by grace you have been saved), and raised us up with Him, and seated us with Him in the heavenly places in Christ Jesus, so that in the ages to come He might show the surpassing riches of His grace in kindness toward us in Christ Jesus. For by grace you have been saved through faith; and that not of yourselves, it is the gift of God; not as a result of works, so that no one may boast. For we are His workmanship, created in Christ Jesus for good works, which God prepared beforehand so that we would walk in them. (Ephesians 2:1–10 NASB)

I have written this devotional in a style that focuses on thoughts for each individual to spend time dwelling and meditating on, being able to memorize those truths that can transform their life walk while in this world as they live from Heaven to earth.

"Being of the same mind, maintaining the same love, united in spirit, intent on one purpose" (Philippians 2:2 NASB).

"And you shall love the Lord your God with all your heart, and with all your soul, and with all your mind, and with all your strength" (Mark 12:30 NASB).

ETERNAL LIFE POINT: The physical moment of now is the greatest opportunity to give expression to the spiritual presence of now!

Concentrate and Meditate on These Words

These words of scripture will be found through this personal study and growing in the mind and heart of Christ Jesus:

Dear friends, listen well to my words. Keep my message in plain view at all times. Concentrate! Learn it by heart! Those who discover these words live, really live; body and soul, they're bursting with health. Keep vigilant watch over your heart; that's where life starts. (Proverbs 4:20–23 Message Bible)

God calls us friends; He has five commands:

1. Listen well to His Words.
2. Tune your ears to His voice.
3. Keep His message in plain view at all times.
4. Concentrate on it (intentional internal focused faith).
5. Learn it by heart (memorize it).

Promise to be fulfilled for those who practice these Words: they will live, really live (abundantly), and their bodies and souls will be bursting with health.

Introduction

Intentional internal focused faith is the heart's matter of truly following Jesus Christ and being able to reflect His image to a world He came to die for and reestablish a Heaven-to-earth relationship with all of humanity again. As I reflect on my years of serving and ministry in the body of Christ, there has been a struggle that appears in the life of many who are the followers of Christ Jesus. I, too, have found myself with this struggle but did not truly understand why. It was not because I myself or because others who were struggling with their walk as followers didn't have heart for following Christ. Heart is a key issue for sure in following after Christ Jesus, but there is a component that plays a great part in becoming a true reflection of the image of Christ for the world He died for. This component is so strong and is the reason why many world-class athletes wear gold rings on their hands or gold medals around their necks or why their fireplace mantles are lined with trophies displaying this one component (and I am not speaking of their pride, although that may be there also), not displayed in rings, gold medals, or trophies but in their personal character.

There is a scripture that can help us discover this component if we are to be the true reflection of Christ Jesus in this world He died for but also remembering in which He created for His pleasures. Every world-class athlete found this component in what was a heart issue of love for them that created the pleasure to be the best they could be. It was no longer about doing the event that would bring them their gold rings, gold necklaces, or trophies; it was about being. That's right—being; being creates this component that many believers have not yet discovered. Listen to this passage of scripture: "So if you're serious about living this new resurrection life with Christ, act like it. Pursue the things over which Christ presides. Don't shuffle along, eyes to the ground, absorbed with the things right in front of you. Look up, and be alert to what is going on around Christ—that's where the action is. See things from his perspective. Your old life is dead. Your new life, which is your real life—even though invisible to spectators—is with Christ in God. He is your life. When Christ (your real life, remember) shows up again on this earth, you'll show up, too—the real you, the glorious you. Meanwhile, be content with obscurity, like Christ" (Colossians 3:1–4 MSG). Now before we look at this scripture in our next chapter, I would like us to look at the opening verse from the New Living Translation: "Since you have been raised to new life with Christ, set your sights on the realities of heaven, where Christ sits in the place of honor at God's right hand" (Colossians 3:1 NLT).

In this one verse, we'll together find this much-needed component that can produce the pleasure our Heavenly Father was looking for when He created you and me. The apostle Paul says to us, "Set your sights (minds) on the realities of heaven." What is he truly talking about here? Our component is found in this statement. Let me ask you a question: how did all those world-class athletes win those gold rings, gold necklaces, and trophies? By setting their sights or minds on the things around them. What was around them? The event they became. What is this statement implying to us who follow Christ Jesus? It is talking about having the mind of Christ, which is intentional internal focused faith, for without this component in our Christian walk, we will struggle at doing the Christian life instead of being the Christian life.

As true followers of Jesus Christ, we are never asked to try or do

Christian acts of serving or ministries, but we are called to be acts of service and ministry. Intentional internal focused faith is the ingredient that is missing in so many of our Christian lives and the key reason for all our struggles in Christ Jesus. It is my heartfelt desire to help and encourage every true follower of Christ Jesus to develop intentional internal focused faith by learning how to set our minds on the things above, where our Savior and Lord is seated at the right hand of our Heavenly Father, as we ourselves are there positioned in and seated in Him (Christ Jesus). "And He raised us up together with Him and made us sit down together [giving us joint seating with Him] in the heavenly sphere [by virtue of our being] in Christ Jesus (the Messiah, the anointed One)" (Ephesians 2:6 AMPC). This is all about a spiritual mindset that is set on the things above, not the things of the earth.

Let's Pray for Our Journey
Father God, we come in the mighty name of our Savior and Lord Jesus Christ asking for pure revelation that we would overcome our lack of intentional internal focused faith on the things above. Teach us to set our minds on the things above and not on the things of the earth that cause us to lose our focus and create the struggles of our lives. Lord Jesus, "therefore we, prepare our minds for action, keeping sober in spirit, fixing our hope completely on the grace to be brought to us at the revelation of Jesus Christ. As obedient children, we will not be conformed to the former lusts which were ours in our ignorance, but like the Holy One who called us, we are to be holy ourselves also in all our behavior; because it is written, 'YOU SHALL BE HOLY, FOR I AM HOLY'" (1 Peter 1:13–16 NASB).

Make each chapter a full week of reflection before moving to the next, learning to be instead of doing. For your being will create the natural flow of doing. Doing never creates being!

Concentrate and Meditate on These Words
Dear friends, listen well to my words. Keep my message in plain view at all times. Concentrate! Learn it by heart! Those who discover these words live, really live; body and soul, they're bursting with health. Keep

vigilant watch over your heart; that's where life starts. (Proverbs 4:20–23 Message Bible)

God calls us friends; He has five commands:

1. Listen well to His Words.
2. Tune your ears to His voice.
3. Keep His message in plain view at all times.
4. Concentrate on it (intentional internal focused faith).
5. Learn it by heart (memorize it).

Promise to be fulfilled for those who practice these Words: they will live, really live (abundantly), and their bodies and souls will be bursting with health.

1. Write for yourself a life application.
2. Memorize the scripture (intentional internal focused faith).
3. Write a prayer from your life application to practice daily.
4. Practice living the truth of your prayer daily.

PRAYING THE MIND AND HEART OF JESUS

Living with and Having the Mind and Heart of Christ Is Every Believer's Responsibility!

Our belief system is built upon what we intentionally focus or set our minds to and intentionally believe in our hearts. It's how we choose to dwell upon the Lord God with our physical being (soul and strength) that determines our level of love for Him.

ETERNAL LIFE POINT: Whatever we as believers do in our minds will be a deciding factor of our belief system from our hearts, affecting our total being (soul and strength). Every believer's mind and heart play a role in how they love the Lord God with all their strength and physical being (soul).

"And you shall love the Lord your God with all your heart, and with all your soul, and with all your mind, and with all your strength" (Mark 12:30 NASB).

Prayer
Lord Jesus, teach me by Your Holy Spirit to truly love You with my total being. Help me to love You with a pure heart that is truly Christ-centered, submitting all my soul to Your calling and choosing me to be covered with Your righteousness and holiness in the truth. Lord, may my mind be intentionally and internally fully focused on living from Heaven to earth with all the strength of my being. Father God, I pray this in Jesus's name, amen.

"For as he thinks within himself, so he is" (Proverbs 23:7 NASB). Heart (kardia) does not refer to the physical organ but is always used figuratively in scripture to refer to the seat and center of human life. The heart refers to the part of a human that controls the desires, emotions, hopes, dreams, and other intangible parts of our being. The mind typically refers to the part of a human that controls the intellect, reason, and thought. No outward obedience is of the slightest value unless the heart and mind are turned to God. The kardia is the seat and center of human life and often referred to as the control center; it's the will of our being. We can make the analogy of the air traffic controllers that monitor and regulate all incoming and outbound traffic at the airport. The significance of the mind and heart in scripture cannot be overestimated. It's imperative for every believer to make an effort to have a basic foundation of scripture's use of the mind and heart.

"Watch over your heart with all diligence, for from it flow the springs of life" (Proverbs 4:23 NASB).

The great Puritan writer John Flavel wrote that "the heart of man is his worst part before it is regenerated, and the best afterward; it is the seat of principles, and the fountain of actions. The eye of God is, and the eye of the Christian ought to be, principally fixed upon it. The greatest difficulty in conversion, is to win the heart to God; and the greatest difficulty after conversion, is to keep the heart with God. Here lies the very force and stress of the Christian life; here is that which makes the way to life a narrow way, and the gate of heaven a strait gate."

ETERNAL LIFE POINT: Where there is no daily practice of renewing the mind and heart, there will always be a struggle for intentional internal focused faith to give a heavenly response to life's circumstances and situations.

ETERNAL LIFE POINT: The keeping and right managing of the mind and heart in our everyday life circumstances and situations is one of the greatest challenges in our Christian life journey.

Proposition
What the philosopher says of waters, is as properly applicable to hearts; it is hard to keep them within any bounds, God has set limits to them, yet how frequently do they transgress not only the bounds of grace and believing faith, but even of reason and common honesty? This is that which affords the Christian matter of labor and watchfulness, to his and her dying day. It is not the cleaning of the hand that makes the

Christian, for many a hypocrite can show as fair a hand as he or she; but the purifying, watching, and right ordering of the heart; this is the thing that provokes so many sad complaints, and costs so many deep groans and tears. It was the pride of Hezekiah's heart that made him lie in the dust, mourning before the Lord. It was the fear of hypocrisy invading the heart that made David cry, "Let my heart be sound in you statutes, that I be not ashamed." It was the sad experience he had of the divisions and distractions of his own heart in the service of God, that made him pour out the prayer, "Unite my heart to fear your name."

Words Reveal Character from the Heart
Either make the tree good and its fruit good, or make the tree bad and its fruit bad; for the tree is known by its fruit. You brood of vipers, how can you, being evil, speak what is good? For the mouth speaks out of that which fills the heart. The good man brings out of his good treasure what is good; and the evil man brings out of his evil treasure what is evil. But I tell you that every careless word that people speak, they shall give an accounting for it in the day of judgment. For by your words you will be justified, and by your words you will be condemned. (Matthew 12:33–37 NASB).

Promise of a New Heart
Moreover, I will give you a new heart and put a new spirit within you; and I will remove the heart of stone from your flesh and give you a heart of flesh. I will put My Spirit within you and cause you to walk in My statutes, and you will be careful to observe My ordinances. (Ezekiel 36:26–27 NASB)

Prayer
Father God, thank You for my new heart of flesh and for removing my old heart of stone. Lord, praise You for giving to me Your Holy Spirit so that I can make choices that honor You and allow heavenly realities to find expression here on earth as I carefully observe Your ordinances while practicing my new being in Christ Jesus, who is my real life. Amen!

Renewing of the Mind Is Our Responsibility
"And do not be conformed to this world, but be transformed by the renewing of your mind, so that you may prove what the will of God is, that which is good and acceptable and perfect" (Romans 12:2 NASB).

"And that you be renewed in the spirit of your mind, and put on the new self, which in the likeness of God has been created in righteousness and holiness of the truth" (Ephesians 4:23–24 NASB).

Prayer
Father God, I thank You that I am a copartner in the divine nature of Christ so that I may practice the renewing of my mind, for I am created in righteousness and holiness of the truth, showing forth that I am an overcomer in Christ Jesus my Lord. Amen!

Your Mind Is the Mind of Christ
"But a natural man does not accept the things of the Spirit of God, for they are foolishness to him; and he cannot understand them, because they are spiritually appraised. But he who is spiritual appraises all things, yet he himself is appraised by no one. FOR WHO HAS KNOWN THE MIND OF THE LORD, THAT HE WILL INSTRUCT HIM? But we have the mind of Christ" (1 Corinthians 2:14–16 NASB).

God's purpose: to encourage each and every believer to grow in their intentional internal focused faith through the renewing of their minds and hearts, believing in Christ Jesus with all their heart as their real life and identity.

Not until we intentionally and internally believe and practice that Christ Jesus is our real life and identity will we overcome our struggle in bringing Heaven's realities to our families and friends on planet earth.

The renewing of our minds starts with our belief system moving from the mindset of the flesh to moving to the mindset of the Spirit. For our belief system f lows from our hearts of actions and behaviors.

ETERNAL LIFE POINT: The intentional internal focused faith of your mind and heart will determine the eternal destiny of your soul.

A Prayer for Intentional Internal Focused Faith: Living from Heaven to Earth!

Promise of a New Heart

"Moreover, I will give you a new heart and put a new spirit within you; and I will remove the heart of stone from your flesh and give you a heart of flesh. I will put My Spirit within you and cause you to walk in My statutes, and you will be careful to observe My ordinances" (Ezekiel 36:26–27 NASB).

Prayer

Father God, thank You for my new heart of flesh and for removing my old heart of stone. Lord, praise You for giving to me Your Holy Spirit so that I can make choices that honor You and allow heavenly realities to find expression here on earth as I carefully observe Your ordinances and practice the renewing of my mind on a daily basis in the truth. Amen!

Renewing of the Mind Is Our Responsibility

"And do not be conformed to this world, but be transformed by the renewing of your mind, so that you may prove what the will of God is, that which is good and acceptable and perfect" (Romans 12:2 NASB).

"And that you be renewed in the spirit of your mind, and put on the new self, which in the likeness of God has been created in righteousness and holiness of the truth" (Ephesians 4:23–24 NASB).

Prayer

Here is a prayer that you can pray on a daily basis for strengthening your spiritual focus:

Father God, I thank You that I am a copartner in the divine nature of Christ so that I may practice the renewing of my mind and the tearing down of my old way of thinking and acting, for I am created in righteousness and holiness of the truth being able to discern and evaluate all my life circumstances and situations that confront me with the mind of Christ Jesus, amen!

We Are Made Complete in Him

"Therefore as you have received Christ Jesus the Lord, so walk in Him, having been firmly rooted and now being built up in Him and established in your faith, just as you were instructed, and overflowing with gratitude. See to it that no one takes you captive through philosophy and empty deception, according to the tradition of men, according to the elementary principles of the world, rather than according to Christ. For in Him all the fullness of Deity dwells in bodily form, and in Him you have been made complete, and He is the head over all rule and authority; and in Him you were also circumcised with a circumcision made without hands, in the removal of the body of the flesh by the circumcision of Christ; having been buried with Him in baptism, in which you were also raised up with Him through faith in the working of God, who raised Him from the dead" (Colossians 2:6–12 NASB).

Prayer

Heavenly Father, I thank You that I have received Christ Jesus and that I now choose to walk in Him. I am being rooted and built up in Him so that I may be established in my growing faith just as I have been instructed and find myself overflowing with gratitude. Help me to watch over my mind so that I would not be taken captive through philosophies and empty deceptions based on the traditions of men, according to the elementary principles of the world rather than according to Jesus, my Lord. Father, all the fullness of Deity dwells in Christ Jesus, to which I am made complete. In Jesus, I have been circumcised, a circumcision made without hands, as Christ Jesus has removed my body of flesh (sin nature) by His death on the cross for me. I am buried with Him and have been raised to a new life in Him as He sits at the right hand of the Father, so I sit in Him. Amen!

We Have the Spirit of God the Father

For to us God revealed (His wisdom) them through the Spirit, for the Spirit searches all things, even the depths of God. For who among men knows the thoughts of a man except the spirit of the man that is in him? Even so, no one knows the thoughts of God except the Spirit of God. Now we have received not the spirit of the world but the Spirit who is from God so that we may know the things freely given to us by God, which are things we also speak not in words taught by human wisdom but in those taught by the Spirit, combining spiritual thoughts with spiritual words.

Prayer

Father, I thank You that You have given to me Your Holy Spirit so that I may know the deep things of Your heart toward me and my circumstances and situations. By Your Spirit, I am able to discern and evaluate and appraise my life circumstances and situations so that I may be able to make Heaven to earth choices that bring glory to Your name, combining spiritual thought with spiritual words; therefore, Heavenly Father, I am able to see and experience the Kingdom's realities all around me while here on earth in every circumstance and every situation that surrounds me. Amen!

But We Have the Mind of Christ

"But a natural man does not accept the things of the Spirit of God, for they are foolishness to him; and he cannot understand them, because they are spiritually appraised. But he who is spiritual appraises all things, yet he himself is appraised by no one. FOR WHO HAS KNOWN THE MIND OF THE LORD, THAT HE WILL INSTRUCT HIM? But we have the mind of Christ" (1 Corinthians 2:10–16 NASB).

Prayer

Lord, how thankful I am for the mind of Christ Jesus, allowing me to focus on the things above and not on the things of the earth. I thank You that because I have the mind of Christ Jesus, I am able to understand the things of the Spirit and have the ability by the Holy Spirit to appraise all things, showing forth the will of my Heavenly Father in my every action and spoken word. Amen!

Focus on the Truth about You

"Rejoice in the Lord always; again I will say, rejoice! Let your gentle spirit be known to all men. The Lord is near. Be anxious for nothing, but in everything by prayer and supplication with thanksgiving let your requests be made known to God. And the peace of God, which surpasses all comprehension, will guard your hearts and your minds in Christ Jesus. Finally, brethren, whatever is true, whatever is honorable, whatever is right, whatever is pure, whatever is lovely, whatever is of good repute, if there is any excellence and if anything worthy of praise, dwell on these things. The things you have learned and received and heard and seen in me, practice these things, and the God of peace will be with you" (Philippians 4:4–9 NASB).

Prayer
Lord God, because I have been given the mind of Christ Jesus, I am able to rejoice always, for I am able to have a quiet and gentle spirit before all men. For I know and truly understand that You are near to me, Father God. Lord, help me to find myself being anxious for nothing but in everything by prayer and supplication with thanksgiving, being able to let my request be made known to You, Heavenly Father. For Your peace, Father God, is able to surpass all my ability to comprehend, guarding my heart and mind in Christ Jesus. Lord, with Your mind in me, I am able to focus on whatever is true, whatever is honorable, whatever is right, whatever is pure, whatever is lovely, whatever is of good repute; I am able to dwell upon whatever is excellent and praiseworthy. Because of my dwelling upon the things above, my Father God of peace will be with me in bringing Heaven's realities to the circumstances and situations that surround my life. Amen!

We Are Copartner in His Divine Nature
"Seeing that His divine power has granted to us everything pertaining to life and godliness, through the true knowledge of Him who called us by His own glory and excellence. For by these He has granted to us His precious and magnificent promises, so that by them you may become partakers of the divine nature, having escaped the corruption that is in the world by lust. Now for this very reason also, applying all diligence, in your faith supply moral excellence, and in your moral

excellence, knowledge, and in your knowledge, self-control, and in your self-control, perseverance, and in your perseverance, godliness, and in your godliness, brotherly kindness, and in your brotherly kindness, love. For if these qualities are yours and are increasing, they render you neither useless nor unfruitful in the true knowledge of our Lord Jesus Christ. For he who lacks these qualities is blind or short-sighted, having forgotten his purification from his former sins. Therefore, brethren, be all the more diligent to make certain about His calling and choosing you; for as long as you practice these things, you will never stumble; for in this way the entrance into the eternal kingdom of our Lord and Savior Jesus Christ will be abundantly supplied to you" (2 Peter 1:3–11 NASB).

Prayer

Lord God, thank You that You have given to me everything pertaining to life and godliness as I grow in the true knowledge of my Lord and Savior, Who has called me by His own glory and excellence. Lord, You have by Your precious and magnificent promises made me a copartner of Your divine nature so that I can escape the corruption that is in the world around me. Lord Jesus, by the enabling empowerment of the Spirit, I can practice with all diligence in my faith, moral excellence, knowledge, self-control, perseverance, godliness, brotherly kindness, and love. Lord, by dwelling on these character traits, I will not be blind or shortsighted but found useful and fruitful in all I do. Father God, thank You that as I practice these qualities, I will never stumble or fall, but the way into the Eternal Kingdom by my Lord and Savior, Jesus Christ, will be abundantly supplied to me. Amen and amen!

Setting My Mind on the Things above, for I Have Been Called for This Purpose

"Therefore if you have been raised up with Christ, keep seeking the things above, where Christ is, seated at the right hand of God. Set your mind on the things above, not on the things that are on earth. For you have died and your life is hidden with Christ in God. When Christ, who is our life, is revealed, then you also will be revealed with Him in glory" (Colossians 3:1–4 NASB).

"For you have been called for this purpose, since Christ also suffered for you, leaving you an example for you to follow in His steps, WHO COMMITTED NO SIN, NOR WAS ANY DECEIT FOUND IN HIS MOUTH; and while being reviled, He did not revile in return; while suffering, He uttered no threats, but kept entrusting Himself to Him who judges righteously; and He Himself bore our sins in His body on the cross, so that we might die to sin and live to righteousness; for by His wounds you were healed" (1 Peter 2:21–24 NASB).

"Therefore, since Christ has suffered in the flesh, arm yourselves also with the same purpose, because he who has suffered in the flesh has ceased from sin, so as to live the rest of the time in the flesh no longer for the lust of men, but for the will of God" (1 Peter 4:1–2 NASB).

Prayer
Father God, because You have raised me up with Christ Jesus, I will practice seeking the things above. For I am dead, hidden in Christ Jesus in You, Father God. Now Jesus is my real life, and I choose to remain in Him until He returns for me, knowing at His return, I then can be seen through His and from His glory.

Father God, You have called and purposed for me to follow after the example of my Lord and Savior, Jesus Christ, who committed no sin, nor was any deceit found in His mouth. While He was being reviled, He did not revile in return; while suffering, He uttered no threats but kept entrusting Himself to You, Father God. Lord, let this be a truthful practice of my life for You today in the behalf of all who come near me today. For by Your wounds, I am healed. Lord, I therefore arm myself to suffer for the sake of Christ Jesus in behalf of others so that they may experience Your heavenly realities for themselves today. For I live for Your will, Father God, to be done on earth as it is in Heaven. Amen and amen!

ETERNAL LIFE POINT: The physical moment of now is the greatest opportunity to give expression to the spiritual presence of now!

Concentrate and Meditate on These Words
Dear friends, listen well to my words. Keep my message in plain view at all times. Concentrate! Learn it by heart! Those who discover these words live, really live; body and soul, they're bursting with health. Keep vigilant [be diligent] watch over your heart; that's where life starts [the issues of life flow from]. (Proverbs 4:20–23 Message Bible)

God calls each of us His friend; He has five commands:

1. Listen well to His Words.
2. Tune your ears to His voice.
3. Keep His message in plain view at all times.
4. Concentrate on it (intentional internal focused faith).
5. Learn it by heart (memorize it).

Promise to be fulfilled for those who practice these Words: they will live, really live (abundantly), and their bodies and souls will be bursting with health.

1. Write for yourself a life application.
2. Memorize the scripture (intentional internal focused faith).
3. Write a prayer from your life application to practice daily.
4. How will you begin to practice living the truth of your prayer daily?

Chapter 1

LEARNING ABOUT POSITION FROM BEING

Since you have been raised to new life with Christ, set your sights on the realities of heaven, where Christ sits in the place of honor at God's right hand. Think about the things of heaven, not the things of earth. For you died to this life, and your real life is hidden with Christ in God. And when Christ, who is your life, is revealed to the whole world, you will share in all his glory.
—Colossians 3:1–4 NLT

Much of my Christian life has been about doing and not about being. And it is here in the doing where most believers in Christ Jesus find themselves. But it is also in this doing relationship why many believers find themselves struggling at maintaining their focus on the things above. I remember as a young believer and in my zeal for the Lord and following after Him that I was so zealously focused on being a follower of Christ Jesus that some of my encouragers thought that I was losing focus on the things of this earth. And one of those well-meaning followers of Christ also said to me, "David, you cannot be so heavenly minded that you do no earthly good." With them being older and much wiser, I thought they were right and began to focus on the things around me, believing that I could do this Christian life stuff as well as all the other stuff around me. WOW, was I ever wrong! Did you know that you cannot do the Christian life? This is why so many followers of Christ Jesus are up and down, over and under, and in and out; they are all about doing. And doing is all about oneself.

The words of my Christian friend and teacher sounded so biblical that I thought this person was truly right—maybe I was being a little too heavenly minded. I was just beginning this Christian journey, so I started watching and listening to those believers who were older and more mature in their Christian walk than I was. It took me a while to learn that not everyone who was older and seemed more mature was walking in victory over the very things I found myself struggling with. How is it that we can tell others how to walk this Christian life and find ourselves still wrestling with issues that we should have been freed from years ago? My friend's advice sounded so good but was so wrong and unscriptural.

Let's listen to the scripture to learn our first lesson on intentional internal focused faith. Here is our first step found in this verse: "Since you have been raised to new life with Christ, set your sights on the realities of heaven, where Christ sits in the place of honor at God's right hand" (Colossians 3:1 NLT). Now there are two very important truths to learn here. First, we must see a truth that does not appear in this verse but is there nevertheless. It's about your belief system! If you are all about the things of the earth, you'll never see the things that are of the heavenly reality. To see the things in the heavenly reality, you must be able to see yourself in Christ Jesus, who is seated at the right hand of your Heavenly Father. The invisible truth is that you must adhere to, trust in, and rely upon your belief in Jesus Christ. If you do not see yourself as raised to a new life with Christ, you will struggle at setting your mind on the reality of Heaven. It is your belief system that allows you the spiritual ability to set your sight (attitude) on the reality of Heaven. You cannot look at the spiritual realm around you until you take your position in Christ Jesus. The writer of Ephesians declares, "For he raised us from the dead along with Christ and seated us with him in the heavenly realms because we are united with Christ Jesus" (Ephesians 2:6 NLT). Do we as believers truly believe this spiritual reality, or are we still bound to this earth suit and its surrounding?

The second truth we have started to touch on is our being in Christ Jesus. Our spiritual position in Christ not only helps us to see the heavenly reality around us but also provides our being and protects us from the power of sin and death that lies around us. The scripture declares, "And because you belong to him, the power of the life-giving Spirit has freed you from the power of sin that leads to death" (Romans 8:2 NAT).

I also like the reading from the New American Standard Bible: "For the law of the Spirit of life in Christ Jesus has set you free from the law of sin and of death" (Romans 8:2 NASB). It again declares our position in Christ Jesus and the life of the Spirit that keep us free from the power of sin and death. Allow me one more scripture to clarify and to back up our being: "For you died to this life, and your real life is hidden with Christ in God. And when Christ, who is your life, is revealed to the whole world, you will share in all his glory" (Colossians 3:3–4 NLT). We now are truly the image of Jesus Christ, for now He is our life while in this world. We are not called to do Christian acts of service, nor are we to be found doing Christian ministries. It's from our *being* that acts of serving and ministering become the natural outflow of who we are, the image of Jesus Christ to our world around us.

Our belief system establishes our ability to have intentional internal focused faith—the component that is much needed in every believer's life journey while on planet earth. We are truly called to live from Heaven to earth not by doing but by being. If you don't understand that, you are not just called to be a Christian; and if you don't understand that Jesus Christ is truly your life, you will continue to do what you have always done from your fallen state in the Garden of Eden. You will live from your external appetite of your fleshly emotions. Adam and Eve failed to believe God and created yours and my fallen lustful appetite, but it was Jesus Christ Who created yours and my spiritual being. What is true of Christ is also true of us in Christ. "Now if we have died with Christ, we believe that we shall also live with Him, knowing that Christ, having been raised from the dead, is never to die again; death no longer is master over Him. For the death that He died, He died to sin once for all; but the life that He lives, He lives to God. Even so consider yourselves to be dead to sin, but alive to God in Christ Jesus" (Romans 6:8–11 NASB).

Let's again listen to the last verse of this scripture: "Even so consider yourselves to be dead to sin, but alive to God in Christ Jesus" (Romans 6:11 NASB). Where are we to live at? In Christ Jesus! Would it not stand to reason that if I am in Christ Jesus my life would be about being rather than about doing? Just like we found ourselves being the recipients of Adam and Eve's fallen state, we now are the recipients of Jesus Christ's resurrection state or being. "As He is so being we in this world" (1 John 4:17).

Let me ask you this question that I often like to ask people. When does an orange become an orange? I love the answer to this question. The orange has always been the orange from its origin within the vine, and now here's what Jesus says about us: "I am the true vine, and My Father is the vinedresser. Every branch in Me that does not bear fruit, He takes away; and every branch that bears fruit, He prunes it so that it may bear more fruit. You are already clean because of the word which I have spoken to you. Abide in Me, and I in you. As the branch cannot bear fruit of itself unless it abides in the vine, so neither can you unless you abide in Me. I am the vine, you are the branches; he who abides in Me and I in him, he bears much fruit, for apart from Me you can do nothing" (John 15:1–5 NASB). Just as the orange matures from abiding in the vine, so do we mature from abiding in the vine as we start being sons and daughters of our Heavenly Father, and it is here that serving and ministering become natural. You see, it's truly not about doing; it's all about being in the image of Christ Jesus. In our next chapter, we will continue our thought line on being. But it's important for us that we take a little at a time. Position and being are essential to intentional internal focused faith. Be encouraged and unafraid of who you are in Christ Jesus.

Concentrate and Meditate on These Words
Dear friends, listen well to my words. Keep my message in plain view at all times. Concentrate! Learn it by heart! Those who discover these words live, really live; body and soul, they're bursting with health. Keep vigilant watch over your heart; that's where life starts. (Proverbs 4:20–23 Message Bible)

God calls us friends; He has five commands:

1. Listen well to His Words.
2. Tune your ears to His voice.
3. Keep His message in plain view at all times.
4. Concentrate on it (intentional internal focused faith).
5. Learn it by heart (memorize it).

Promise to be fulfilled for those who practice these Words: they will live, really live (abundantly), and their bodies and souls will be bursting with health.

1. Write for yourself a life application.
2. Memorize the scripture (intentional internal focused faith).
3. Write a prayer from your life application to practice daily.
4. Practice living the truth of your prayer daily.

Chapter 2

YOUR REAL LIFE IS HIDDEN

For you died to this life, and your real life is hidden with Christ in God.
—Colossians 3:3 NLT
"Only those who can see the invisible can do the impossible."
ETERNAL LIFE POINT: Only those who remain hidden in Christ
will experience their real life—Christ Jesus.

Who do you see the real you to be? It has been said that there are three
views to every person: what they see themselves to be, what others
around them see them to be, and what God sees them to be. If we do
not have the right view or perspective of ourselves, we will never be
able to grow in our intentional focused faith. This is why it is so vitally
important to have a clear view of God's heavenly perspective of you.
Listen again to our opening verse in this chapter: "For you died to this
life, and your real life is hidden with Christ in God." Do we understand
that what we think is our life isn't our life and what we don't think is
our life is our real life?

We have to stop focusing on these physical bodies of ours—that is, the physical nature of it—and start to focus on the spiritual beings we are in these physical bodies. There is still too much emphasis on the physical earth suit that we are not putting to death. Scripture encourages us by saying, "For if you are living according to the flesh, you must die; but if by the Spirit you are putting to death the deeds of the body, you will live" (Romans 8:13 NASB).

Because of the wrong emphasis given to this earth suit, many believers are more about doing than about being. Being is about the natural process of becoming in the image of Jesus Christ, and doing is about performing into something that only lasts for a moment of time (like a false image) only to find yourself having to struggle at doing it all over again. You're just never able to reach that level that's good enough. We often become discouraged, frustrated, and ready to give up or just settle for "this is the way it is" attitude.

Scripture gives us some wonderful pictures of who we are in Christ Jesus. But if we are to have clear intentional focused faith about ourselves and be able to see the true beings we are in Christ, we need to be clear in our thinking. Changing the way we think is not as easy as it may sound. Maybe it's one of the most difficult habits to learn and practice. The renewing of our minds is the most important principle of learning the true identity of the real you. Did you know that the scripture declares you and I to be complete already? In Colossians 2:9–10, these powerful words are stated: "For in Him all the fullness of Deity dwells in bodily form, and in Him you have been made complete, and He is the head over all rule and authority" (Colossians 2:9–10 NASB).

The Word of God is talking about your identity, your covering, and your completion in Christ Jesus. Yet if you and I are always focused on the outside of the earth suit, we'll continually wrestle with the imperfections and falsifying of who we are. Please listen carefully to these words: "For in Him all the fullness of Deity dwells." This means the Father, Son, and Holy Spirit are all in one the Son, and now you and I have been made complete in Him (Christ Jesus), Who is the Father, Son, and Holy Spirit. This is the real you and your real life. "Your old life is dead. Your new life, which is your real life—even though invisible to spectators—is with Christ in God. He is your life. When Christ (your real life, remember) shows up again on this earth, you'll show up, too—the real you, the glorious you. Meanwhile, be content with obscurity, like Christ" (Colossians 3:3–4 MSG).

That's it, isn't it? Being content with obscurity, really, not on my shift, it's all about me and how I desire my life to be and to turn out for me. Here again is our struggle at renewing our minds, because we can't just stop thinking about ourselves. We find this to be the reason why so many people continually return to their old patterns of habits or behaviors. This is even true for sincere believers who long to overcome their battles with their fleshly appetites. We fail to believe the Word of God through the renewing of our minds.

Do you believe what you read, or do you read what you believe? Scripture once again says and encourages us with these most powerful words: "By his divine power, God has given us everything we need for living a godly life. We have received all of this by coming to know him, the one who called us to himself by means of his marvelous glory and excellence. And because of his glory and excellence, he has given us great and precious promises. These are the promises that enable you to share his divine nature and escape the world's corruption caused by human desires" (2 Peter 1:3–4 NLT). I cannot practice what I do not believe about myself; why? Because how I see myself is what I practice. Our orange never struggles with or wrestles with its identity because it remains hidden in the vine until its real life is to be revealed.

Sometimes when hearing something that sounds right and feels good, it can give an individual a sense of false security and a false belief about themselves. How many times have you, as well as myself, heard a solid word of encouragement? It was just what we needed to hear, and we truly felt and believed it was true and we had it. Only to find what we thought was true and right, within a matter of moments, an hour or even a period of time had passed, but now we struggle at thinking that word was ever true at all. This is all about our ability to have single-minded focus.

There is a phrase found in the book of Philippians that is spoken of to the Body of Christ that can also speak to us individually, as well as the whole: "Then make me truly happy by agreeing wholeheartedly with each other, loving one another, and working together with one mind and purpose" (Philippians 2:2 NLT). Did you see the phrase "working together with one mind and purpose"? Many of us are not-single minded, nor do we have a single purpose for our lives. The reason for this has much to do with our wholeheartedness that's wrapped up in our belief system about our true identity. The real you is to remain hidden until the return of our Savior and Lord in His glory. "And when Christ, who is your life, is revealed to the whole world, you will share in all his glory" (Colossians 3:4 NLT). So who am I until then? We'll look more into that in the next chapter. Only those hidden in Christ can see the invisible and become the impossible!

Life Application

1. In this search for the real you, what stands out about your struggle to finding the real you?
2. Why is it so important to have single-mindedness?
3. Are there or has there been times you received a good encouragement only to find yourself failing to practice it? Why do you think that is?
4. What's an important life application here for you?

Concentrate and Meditate on These Words

Dear friends, listen well to my words. Keep my message in plain view at all times. Concentrate! Learn it by heart! Those who discover these words live, really live; body and soul, they're bursting with health. Keep vigilant watch over your heart; that's where life starts. (Proverbs 4:20–23 Message Bible)

God calls us friends; He has five commands:

1. Listen well to His Words.
2. Tune your ears to His voice.
3. Keep His message in plain view at all times.
4. Concentrate on it (intentional internal focused faith).
5. Learn it by heart (memorize it).

Promise to be fulfilled for those who practice these Words: they will live, really live (abundantly), and their bodies and souls will be bursting with health.

Chapter 3

WHO'S YOUR REAL LIFE?

Your old life is dead. Your new life, which is your real life—even though invisible to spectators—is with Christ in God. He is your life. When Christ (your real life, remember) shows up again on this earth, you'll show up, too—the real you, the glorious you. Meanwhile, be content with obscurity, like Christ.
—Colossians 3:3–4 MSG

"There is no eternal life without Christ as your real life!"

How does anyone remain in obscurity and let someone else live in their place? Haven't all of us, at one time or another, believed that life was about us? Our days started with and ended with us. We were brought into this world so that everyone could enjoy us and for us anything their hearts want to do for us. We couldn't believe that people around us could truly handle life without us in their lives. Besides, those around us were created for our happiness and pleasures. Anyone's existence was for the purpose of fulfilling our dreams, and they just couldn't handle life on their own without our presence. Wow! Maybe I should stop right here before you start believing that I am talking about myself—imagine that.

This, too, is a mindset or attitude that all of us—at one time or another—displayed and lived out. Maybe you would describe this mindset in a different way, but nevertheless, it's all about one's self-centeredness and playing the role of God. We would never openly declare that or even admit it. But it's true; just like Adam and Eve in the garden, we continue to listen to the voice that says, "You surely will not die! For God knows that in the day you eat from it your eyes will be opened, and you will be like God, knowing good and evil" (Genesis 3:4–5 NASB). Will there ever come a time in our lives that we'll stop trying to improve or change who we are and discover that in Christ Jesus we are made complete already? It's not about improving or changing; it's all about maturing and growing into the real person we are in Christ, Who is our real life.

In the book of Colossians, a verse of scripture stands out here; just listen quietly to these words: "And you are in Him, made full and having come to fullness of life [in Christ you too are filled with the Godhead—Father, Son and Holy Spirit—and reach full spiritual stature]. And He is the Head of all rule and authority [of every angelic principality and power]" (Colossians 2:10 AMPC). This may be hard for you to understand, but understand we must. Every born-again believer is made complete in Jesus Christ right at the moment of their spiritual birth. What is not completed is the maturity and growth of every believer. Maturity and growth come by the intentional internal focused faith of each and every believer. Being able to understand that Jesus Christ is our real life is not what many are being taught or encouraged to focus on and believe. Most of our Christian walk is based upon becoming something or doing something that causes us to work or perform ourselves into the image of Christ Jesus. Here we find that the scripture declares us as being complete already in Christ Jesus.

So let's explore this verse by asking ourselves the question, What is it of us that is made complete in Christ Jesus? The verse declares, "And you are in Him, made full [complete] and having come to fullness of life." I have not found nor have I shared life with any believer who finds themselves as full and complete as believers. If anything is said or spoken of about their Christian journey, it is often in the fact that "I am still a sinner, and so I go by His grace." I understand what is being said here, for I have felt and said this also. But with all my heart, I believe it's statements like this that keep us blinded to our real life—Christ Jesus. Our completion is found here in our position. The Word says, "And you are in Him." What is there of Christ that is not complete? If you said nothing, you are right, for everything was made by Him and through Him and for Him.

Here is a passage of scripture that speaks of Christ whom you and I find ourselves hidden in: "[Now] He is the exact likeness of the unseen God [the visible representation of the invisible]; He is the Firstborn of all creation. For it was in Him that all things were created, in heaven and on earth, things seen and things unseen, whether thrones, dominions, rulers, or authorities; all things were created and exist through Him [by His service, intervention] and in and for Him. And He Himself existed before all things, and in Him all things consist (cohere, are held together) [Proverbs 8:22–31]" (Colossians 1:15–17 AMPC).

Truly, what is it that we think we must become before we can honestly declare ourselves fully complete in the full image of our Savior and Lord? The answer to our question, What is it of us that is made complete in Christ Jesus? It's our spiritual person! As we seek to choose the Lord each day, it's necessary to remember that each and every one of us has a desire to follow our flesh and think or do whatever feels right or seems easiest for ourselves. As Paul spoke so clearly in Romans 8, for those who are outside of Christ, there is no choice. They are controlled completely by their sinful flesh. Believers, Paul says, have the Holy Spirit living within them. By the Spirit, we are becoming more and more like Jesus. The Holy Spirit gives us the power to overcome our flesh. "Therefore, dear brothers and sisters, you have no obligation to do what your sinful nature urges you to do" (Romans 8:12 NLT).

As Paul told the believers, we can choose. "For if you live by its dictates, you will die. But if through the power of the Spirit you put to death the deeds of your sinful nature, you will live. For all who are led by the Spirit of God are children of God" (Romans 8:13–14 NLT).

What if each one of us would choose right from the start of our day, especially first thing in the morning, to set our minds on the Holy Spirit? It's true that if you're anything like I am, I usually spend a few minutes gathering my thoughts for the day before I get out of bed in the morning. Again, it is in these eternal moments that it can become a temptation to choose to think first about our day, our schedule, what we need to do, and who needs to be where; and once we establish our schedules, before we know it, we can fall prey to the lies of the enemy and begin dreading our day or feeling overwhelmed by it and then try to tackle it as soon as our feet hit the floor. What if, instead, you and I were to choose to die for the sake of Christ? What if, by God's grace, we would choose to fight our sinful flesh, put it to death as God's Word instructs us, and set our minds on His way instead of allowing our thoughts to run amok? What if we were to put Christ first, our mate second, our children third, others next, and then our ministries and work? Practically speaking, what would this look like? We would begin by thanking the Lord for the gift of a new day and acknowledge that He alone is sovereign and that He alone is in control—not us. And then by His grace, we would put aside our thoughts, our concerns, and our agendas and draw near to God by spending time in His Word and in prayer. No matter how much we think about our day or our agenda, the reality is that the day belongs to the Lord. If we start each day with intentional internal focused faith and acknowledging this and acknowledging who we are in Christ, this practice could easily transform how we think about and live out the rest of the eternal moments in the day.

Life Application

1. What would you say has been or is your main focus when you start your day?
2. How do you feel about the thought of living your life in obscurity and letting Christ live in your place?

3. What might be different in your situation if you had or would let Christ be your life?
4. What one practical change do you need to make for Christ to live in your place?
5. Pray and ask your Heavenly Father for the courage to remain hidden in Christ, Who is your real life, until His return.
6. Memorize those verses that will establish your being in Him.

Concentrate and Meditate on These Words

Dear friends, listen well to my words. Keep my message in plain view at all times. Concentrate! Learn it by heart! Those who discover these words live, really live; body and soul, they're bursting with health. Keep vigilant watch over your heart; that's where life starts. (Proverbs 4:20–23 Message Bible)

God calls us friends; He has five commands:

1. Listen well to His Words.
2. Tune your ears to His voice.
3. Keep His message in plain view at all times.
4. Concentrate on it (intentional internal focused faith).
5. Learn it by heart (memorize it).

Promise to be fulfilled for those who practice these Words: they will live, really live (abundantly), and their bodies and souls will be bursting with health.

Chapter 4

JUSTIFICATION CREATES BEING!

Justify to Be!

I am the true grapevine, and my Father is the gardener. He cuts off every branch of mine that doesn't produce fruit, and he prunes the branches that do bear fruit so they will produce even more. You have already been pruned and purified by the message I have given you. Remain in me, and I will remain in you. For a branch cannot produce fruit if it is severed from the vine, and you cannot be fruitful unless you remain in me. "Yes, I am the vine; you are the branches. Those who remain in me, and I in them, will produce much fruit. For apart from me you can do nothing."
— John 15:1–5 NLT

ETERNAL LIFE POINT: Position creates being, and being establishes the creative flow of fruit bearing.

A Reason for Everything

He must be received in heaven, you see, until the time which God spoke about through the mouth of his holy prophets from ancient days, the time when God will restore all things.
—Acts 3: 21

Christ's Death and Resurrection Started Our Restoration of Being!

"It is possible to heal the mind, the brain, and the body. We can retell our story and change our future. We can change the impact that the past has on us. This is called retroactive causation in quantum physics" (Dr. Caroline Leaf, *Switch On Your Brain*). Sometimes looking at the world around us or even looking at our own lives, it seems that things will never change. The world will always be a mess, and our lives will always be a mess. We will always be sick, tired, and sad. But today, you and I can choose to believe that everything will always stay the same, or you and I can choose to believe that things can change. That change is possible. We have the wonderful gift to choose to believe in God's promise that He will restore all things under Heaven and earth.

ETERNAL LIFE POINT: The ingredients of your future already exist. God can, and will, restore yours and my life and the world around each of us. True healing is not only possible with God but also promised by God! Remember, God is not bound by time; the ingredients of your future already exist in Christ Jesus.

Let's Understand Our Justification
In Christian theology, justification is God's act of removing the guilt and penalty of sin while at the same time making a sinner righteous through Christ's atoning sacrifice. Why is justification by faith such an important doctrine?

ETERNAL LIFE POINT: Justification by faith is the only means by which a person will enter the Kingdom of God. For justification creates being, and being establishes the natural flow of doing or fruit bearing!

Life-Changing Point for Living in Our Freedom God's purpose: to show that after accepting Jesus Christ by faith (a believing with your heart and a confessing with your mouth) to return to any form of work or performance to keep the faith is actually a nullification of the faith.

Fruit bearing is a natural process to the tree or vine to which the branch is attached. You never see the branches of any fruit-bearing tree or fruit-bearing vine staining or struggling to produce what is natural to its existence.

Listening to Scripture
"Are you so foolish and so senseless and so silly? Having begun [your new life spiritually] with the [Holy] Spirit, are you now reaching perfection [by dependence] on the flesh?" (Galatians 3:3 AMPC). "How foolish can you be? After starting your new lives in the Spirit, why are you now trying to become perfect by your own human effort?" (Galatians 3:3 NLT).

"For in Christ lives all the fullness of God in a human body. So you also are complete through your union with Christ, who is the head over every ruler and authority. When you came to Christ, you were "circumcised," but not by a physical procedure. Christ performed a spiritual circumcision—the cutting away of your sinful nature" (Colossians 2:9–11 NLT).

"If then you have been raised with Christ [to a new life, thus sharing His resurrection from the dead], aim at and seek the [rich, eternal treasures] that are above, where Christ is, seated at the right hand of God [Psalm 110:1]. And set your minds and keep them set on what is above (the higher things), not on the things that are on the earth. For [as far as this world is concerned] you have died, and your [new, real] life is hidden with Christ in God. When Christ, who is our life, appears, then you also will appear with Him in [the splendor of His] glory" (Colossians 3:1–4 AMPC).

"And He raised us up together with Him and made us sit down together [giving us joint seating with Him] in the heavenly sphere [by virtue of our being] in Christ Jesus (the Messiah, the anointed One)" (Ephesians 2:6 AMPC).

Answer: The teaching of justification by faith is what separates biblical Christianity from all other belief systems. In every religion and in some branches of what is called Christianity, man is working his way to God. Only in true biblical Christianity is man saved as a result of grace through faith. Only when we get back to the Bible do we see that justification is by faith, apart from works.

ETERNAL LIFE POINT: The work for our eternal salvation is established and sealed by the blood and work of Jesus Christ on the cross, and nothing we do can ever change that, for we are God's good work in Christ Jesus. Therefore, we are made complete already in Him.

"And I am convinced and sure of this very thing, that He Who began a good work in you will continue until the day of Jesus Christ [right up to the time of His return], developing [that good work] and perfecting and bringing it to full completion in you" (Philippians 1:6 AMPC).

ETERNAL LIFE POINT: Our Father God is forever pruning us for His good works of natural fruit bearing.

The word *justified* means "pronounced or treated as righteous." For a Christian, justification is the act of God not only forgiving the believer's sins but also imputing to him the righteousness of Christ. The Bible states in several places that justification only comes through faith (e.g., Romans 5:1, Galatians 3:24). Justification is not earned through our own works; rather, we are covered by the righteousness of Jesus Christ (Ephesians 2:8, Titus 3:5). The Christian, being declared righteous, is thus freed from the guilt of sin.

"For it is by free grace (God's unmerited favor) that you are saved (delivered from judgment and made partakers of Christ's salvation) through [your] faith. And this [salvation] is not of yourselves [of your own doing, it came not through your own striving], but it is the gift of God; for we are God's [own] handiwork (His workmanship), recreated in Christ Jesus, [born anew] that we may do those good works which God predestined (planned beforehand) for us [taking paths which He prepared ahead of time], that we should walk in them [living the good life which He prearranged and made ready for us to live]" (Ephesians 2:8, 10 AMPC).

Justification is a completed work of God, and it is instantaneous, as opposed to sanctification, which is an ongoing process of growth by which we become more Christ-like (the act of being saved, cf. 1 Corinthians 1:18, 1 Thessalonians 5:23). Sanctification occurs after justification.

Understanding the doctrine of justification is important for a Christian. First, it is the very knowledge of justification and of grace that motivates our position of being. Good work is a natural process of spiritual growth (not doing or performing good works but being good works themselves) because good work is natural by produce of who we are in Christ Jesus; thus, justification leads to sanctification. Also, the fact that justification is a finished work of God means that Christians have assurance of their salvation; they do not have to work for it for them to experience Heaven. In God's eyes, believers have the righteousness necessary to gain eternal life.

This speaks to the believer's position and identity in Christ Jesus. Once a person is justified, there is nothing else he needs in order to gain entrance into heaven. Since justification comes by faith in Christ, based on His work on our behalf, our own works are disqualified as a means of salvation (Romans 3:28). There exist vast religious systems with complex theologies that teach the false doctrine of justification by works. But they are teaching "a different gospel—which is really no gospel at all" (Galatians 1:6–7).

Without an understanding of justification by faith alone, we cannot truly perceive the glorious gift of grace—God's unmerited favor becomes merited in our minds, and we begin to think we deserve salvation. The doctrine of justification by faith helps us maintain "pure devotion to Christ" (2 Corinthians 11:3). Holding to justification by faith keeps us from falling for the lie that we can earn Heaven. There is no ritual, no sacrament, and no deed that can make us worthy of the righteousness of Christ. It is only by His grace, in response to our faith, that God has credited to us the holiness of His Son. Both Old and New Testaments say, "The just shall live by faith" (Habakkuk 2:4, Romans 1:17, Galatians 3:11, Hebrews 10:38).

The obvious impossibility of carrying out such a moral program should make it plain that no one can sustain a relationship with God that way. The person who lives in the right relationship with God does it by embracing what God arranges for him. Doing things for God is the opposite of entering what God does for you.

Habakkuk had it right: "The person who believes God, is set right by God—and that's the real life."

Rule-keeping does not naturally evolve into living by faith but only perpetuates itself in more and more rule-keeping, a fact observed in scripture: "The one who does these things [rule-keeping] continues to live by them" (Galatians 3:11–12 MSG).

ETERNAL LIFE POINT: Every believer who lives in the right relationship with God does it by embracing what God arranges and has done for him or her through Christ Jesus.

It's all about faith! You have to choose to believe this healing is possible. You decide what kind of world you want to live for; you decide what kind of reality you are going to create. You can retell your story—you are not bound by your past.

Life-Changing Point for Living in Our Freedom: You and I are the creation of God's good works in Christ Jesus (our justification), and we as branches are connected to the true vine through which good works are a natural fruit to the world around each one of us.

Life Application

1. What stands out to you in this thought line of justification?
2. Why do you find it hard to believe in your justification?

3. How does understanding that you are justified in the works of Christ Jesus change how you live your life for Him?

4. What's your life application from this study going to look like in your eternal moment?

5. Memorize those verses that will help you bear the fruit that is natural to the branch as it abides in the vine.

Concentrate and Meditate on These Words

Dear friends, listen well to my words. Keep my message in plain view at all times. Concentrate! Learn it by heart! Those who discover these words live, really live; body and soul, they're bursting with health. Keep vigilant watch over your heart; that's where life starts. (Proverbs 4:20–23 Message Bible)

God calls us friends; He has five commands:

1. Listen well to His Words.
2. Tune your ears to His voice.
3. Keep His message in plain view at all times.
4. Concentrate on it (intentional internal focused faith).
5. Learn it by heart (memorize it),

Promise to be fulfilled for those who practice these Words: they will live, really live (abundantly), and their bodies and souls will be bursting with health.

Chapter 5

CRUCIFIED TO THE WORLD

ETERNAL LIFE POINT: Only those who live for the sake of Jesus Christ can die for the life of another.

What does this thought—"Crucified to the World"—have to do with my intentional focused faith?

Have you ever tried to teach a child to ride a bike? You must help them to focus their attention on what they are doing and keep them from focusing on what is not happening or going to happen while starting to learn to control their abilities to focus on riding and enjoying their ability to ride. You and I must see that the child's ability to ride is already there within him or her. Our goal is to help them have intentional focus on riding.

Our spiritual ability to have intentional focused faith on crucifying ourselves to the world is a lot like trying to ride a bike for the first time. We focus on all the things we don't want to happen to us as we get on the bike (we are sure we can't do this, we don't want to fall, how do we steer and pedal at the same time, how do we balance ourselves without falling and crashing—hurting ourselves and others?)

Scripture declares, "But may it never be that I would boast, except in the cross of our Lord Jesus Christ, through which the world has been crucified to me, and I to the world" (Galatians 6:14 NASB).

Do we know and understand that until the world is crucified to us and we to the world, we who believe will never truly experience the empowerment of the resurrection and infilling of the Holy Spirit so that we may overcome the lustful appetite of our sinful flesh? Living and dying for the sake of Jesus Christ in behalf of another is the beginning of which the world has been crucified to us and us to this world.

It is here that others see the image of Christ Jesus as we allow Him to live in our place. The apostle Peter says it like this: "For you have been called for this purpose, since Christ also suffered for you, leaving you an example for you to follow in His steps, who committed no sin, nor was any deceit found in His mouth; and while being reviled, He did not revile in return; while suffering, He uttered no threats, but kept entrusting Himself to Him who judges righteously; and He Himself bore our sins in His body on the cross, so that we might die to sin and live to righteousness; for by His wounds you were healed" (1 Peter 2:21–24 NASB).

We have a purpose and calling to follow the example of our Lord, and it's in our obedience of doing so that we'll experience healing for our obedience to live like Christ Jesus. Unless you are intentionally focused on living for the sake of Christ Jesus, you'll always be living for yourself and not for others. Our intentional focus as believers is to live in this eternal moment of now.

Here again we are talking about Jesus Christ Who is eternal life. Scripture so encourages us, "Those who belong to Christ Jesus have nailed the passions and desires of their sinful nature to his cross and crucified them there. Since we are living by the Spirit, let us follow the Spirit's leading in every part of our lives" (Galatians 5:24–25 NLT).

"Great faith is a product of great fights. Great testimonies are the outcome of great tests. Great triumphs can only come out of great trials" (Smith Wigglesworth).

I am not sure how many of us as believers really and truly understand that we are called to die and live for the sake of Christ Jesus on a daily basis. Jesus Himself said it so clearly, "And He said to all, if any person wills to come after Me, let him deny himself [disown himself, forget, lose sight of himself and his own interests, refuse and give up himself] and take up his cross daily and follow Me [cleave steadfastly to Me, conform wholly to My example in living and, if need be, in dying also]. For whoever would preserve his life and save it will lose and destroy it, but whoever loses his life for My sake, he will preserve and save it [from the penalty of eternal death]" (Luke 9:23–24 AMPC).

Did you notice that He says wills to come after Him? There are many who would declare themselves to be followers of Christ Jesus but their lifestyle declares they are still living for the sake of self-preservation. Anxiety is worry and another form of fear. It is a care or concern for something to the extent that it disturbs or troubles our soul. It is taking thought to something so much that it encumbers our mind. Anxiety causes fear, sorrow, fretting, and dread because we believe that God will not care for our situation appropriately. Listen to the words of Jesus: "That is why I tell you not to worry about everyday life—whether you have enough food and drink, or enough clothes to wear. Isn't life more than food, and your body more than clothing? Look at the birds. They don't plant or harvest or store food in barns, for your heavenly Father feeds them. And aren't you far more valuable to him than they are? Can all your worries add a single moment to your life? And why worry about your clothing? Look at the lilies of the field and how they grow. They don't work or make their clothing, yet Solomon in all his glory was not dressed as beautifully as they are. And if God cares so wonderfully for wildflowers that are here today and thrown into the fire tomorrow, he will certainly care for you. Why do you have so little faith? So don't worry about these things, saying, 'What will we eat? What will we drink? What will we wear?' These things dominate the thoughts of unbelievers, but your heavenly Father already knows all your needs. Seek the Kingdom of God above all else, and live righteously, and he will give you everything you need. So don't worry about tomorrow, for tomorrow will bring its own worries. Today's trouble is enough for today" (Matthew 6:25–34 NLT).

Here is one of the greatest examples of living for oneself. Did you take note that the denying of oneself means to disown oneself, forget, lose sight of oneself and one's own interests, refuse, and give up oneself? Luke 9:23–24 is about intentional internal focused faith, and Matthew 6:25–34 is the practical application of Luke 9:23–24.

I love how Jesus states clearly that it's an everyday choice to take one's cross, which is implying a denial of oneself and choosing to live for His sake in the eternal moment of now. We cannot start this devotion to Him and the Kingdom and righteousness at the end of our day—after we have taken care of all our issues and concerns in the day then turn and look at what might be His concerns for our lives as we are getting ready to lay our heads down for a night sleep. This intentional internal focused faith is all about living for the sake of Christ Jesus in every matter that concerns and touches our life from the beginning to the ending of our day.

Life Application for the Week

1. Why do you find it hard to die for others for the sake of Christ?
2. What must you do to live for the sake of Christ Jesus in behalf of others?
3. What verse of scripture can you memorize that will help you have intentional internal focused faith here?
4. Write a life application for yourself to be crucified to this world, living for the sake of Christ Jesus in behalf of others.

Concentrate and Meditate on These Words

Dear friends, listen well to my words. Keep my message in plain view at all times. Concentrate! Learn it by heart! Those who discover these words live, really live; body and soul, they're bursting with health. Keep vigilant watch over your heart; that's where life starts. (Proverbs 4:20–23 Message Bible)

God calls us friends; He has five commands:

1. Listen well to His Words.
2. Tune your ears to His voice.
3. Keep His message in plain view at all times.
4. Concentrate on it (intentional internal focused faith).
5. Learn it by heart (memorize it).

Promise to be fulfilled for those who practice these Words: they will live, really live (abundantly), and their bodies and souls will be bursting with health.

Chapter 6

LIVING FOR THE SAKE OF CHRIST

(Dying to Live)

ETERNAL LIFE POINT: The physical moment of now is the greatest opportunity to give expression to the spiritual presence of now!

Building Intentional Internal Focused Faith
"If you acknowledge and confess with your lips that Jesus is Lord and in your heart believe (adhere to, trust in, and rely on the truth) that God raised Him from the dead, you will be saved. For with the heart a person believes (adheres to, trusts in, and relies on Christ) and so is justified (declared righteous, acceptable to God), and with the mouth he confesses (declares openly and speaks out freely his faith) and confirms [his] salvation" (Romans 10:9–10 AMPC).

Two Ways of Receiving the Gospel
Intellectualizing or internalizing. Intellectualizing is created by being able to make sense of what is trying to be understood through the natural mind by processing through our external emotions (it's all about facts; this is

the mindset of the flesh). Internalizing is through the mindset of the Spirit, believing with the heart of faith or belief that creates adherence to a trusting in and a relying on spiritual truth that establishes the Kingdom's realities in the life of a believer.

Introduction

You know airplanes take off every day. All around the world people fasten their seatbelts and let a complete stranger take them thirty-two thousand feet in the air. You also know the vast majority survive. With your feet on the ground, you say, "I believe I would survive if I flew on an airplane." Is this how you define belief?

Many people believe Jesus Christ really exists. Many believe He is Who He claimed to be—God Himself and the savior of the world. But that's not biblical faith; that's just mental assent—an acceptance of the facts. The Bible says demons "believe" in this way (James 2:19).

"You believe that God is one; you do well. So do the demons believe and shudder [in terror and horror such as make a man's hair stand on end and contract the surface of his skin]! Are you willing to be shown [proof], you foolish (unproductive, spiritually deficient) fellow, that faith apart from [good] works is inactive and ineffective and worthless?" (James 2:19–20 AMPC).

Biblical faith is very different. Biblical faith goes beyond mental acceptance of the facts. Biblical faith is like actually buying a ticket. Biblical faith is like boarding a plane, fastening your seat belt, and trusting that pilot to take you up and back down again. Biblical faith is trust—putting your eternal destiny in the hands of this Jesus Who claims to be the only savior of the world.

Jesus said in John 5:24, "Truly, truly, I say to you, he who hears my word, and believes him who sent me, has eternal life, and does not come into judgment, but has passed out of death into life." One who believes in this way is trusting Jesus Christ with his eternal destiny. More than sixty times, the New Testament tells us eternal life is given to those who put their faith (trust) in Christ alone for salvation.

To believe or have faith in Jesus Christ means "adhere to, we obey, nothing can separate us from Christ"; it means we have complete faith or absolute trust in God. And rely upon means we are not self-sufficient but God is our sufficiency.

Without this understanding of the word *believe*, we may have only an intellectual acknowledgment of God. This is the beginning of learning to die to self.

i.   ETERNAL LIFE POINT: There is no Kingdom life without death. One must die first in order to enter the Kingdom of God.

"Now there was a certain man among the Pharisees named Nicodemus, a ruler (a leader, an authority) among the Jews, who came to Jesus at night and said to Him, rabbi, we know and are certain that you have come from God [as] a teacher; for no one can do these signs (these wonderworks, these miracles—and produce the proofs) that you do unless God is with him. Jesus answered him, I assure you, most solemnly I tell you, that unless a person is born again (anew, from above), he cannot ever see (know, be acquainted with, and experience) the kingdom of God. Nicodemus said to Him, how can a man be born when he is old? Can he enter his mother's womb again and be born? Jesus answered, I assure you, most solemnly I tell you, unless a man is born of water and [even] the Spirit, he cannot [ever] enter the kingdom of God [Ezekiel 36:25–27]" (John 3:1–5 AMPC).

How does one become born of the Spirit?

ETERNAL LIFE POINT: In becoming a believer and a follower in Jesus Christ, death is not optional; it's a requirement!

"And He said to all, if any person wills to come after Me, let him deny himself [disown himself, forget, lose sight of himself and his own interests, refuse and give up himself] and take up his cross daily and follow Me [cleave steadfastly to Me, conform wholly to My example in living and, if need be, in dying also]. For whoever would preserve his life and save it will lose and destroy it, but whoever loses his life for My sake, he will preserve and save it [from the penalty of eternal death]" (Luke 9:23–24 AMPC).

It is a requirement to die to self in order to follow after Christ Jesus, for there is only death for those who do not follow after Him—eternal death.

What is it that we are putting to death? ("Disown himself, forget, lose sight of himself and his own interests, refuse and give up himself.")

"For those who are according to the flesh and are controlled by its unholy desires set their minds on and pursue those things which gratify the flesh, but those who are according to the Spirit and are controlled by the desires of the Spirit set their minds on and seek those things which gratify the [Holy] Spirit" (Romans 8:5 AMPC).

"So then, brethren, we are debtors, but not to the flesh [we are not obligated to our carnal nature], to live [a life ruled by the standards set up by the dictates] of the flesh. For if you live according to [the dictates of] the flesh, you will surely die. But if through the power of the [Holy] Spirit you are [habitually] putting to death (making extinct, deadening) the [evil] deeds prompted by the body, you shall [really and genuinely] live forever" (Romans 8:12–13 AMPC).

ETERNAL LIFE POINT: It is the believer's daily conscious choice and habitual and continual practice of putting to death their deeds of the flesh that establish their walking by the life of the Holy Spirit.

ii. Living with the mind of Christ is a prerequisite for understanding the heart of God.

We do and say what we believe. And all our doing and all our saying come from our mindset. Scripture declares, "As a man thinks in his heart, so is he."

Here is Jesus's statement about the heart:

"And He said, what comes out of a man is what makes a man unclean and renders [him] unhallowed. For from within, [that is] out of the hearts of men, come base and wicked thoughts, sexual immorality, stealing, murder, adultery, Coveting (a greedy desire to have more wealth), dangerous and destructive wickedness, deceit; unrestrained (indecent) conduct; an evil eye (envy), slander (evil speaking, malicious misrepresentation, abusiveness), pride (the sin of an uplifted heart against God and man), foolishness (folly, lack of sense, recklessness, thoughtlessness). All these evil [purposes and desires] come from within, and they make the man unclean and render him unhallowed" (Mark 7:20–23 AMPC).

All this is what changes when we ask Christ into our hearts as we set our minds on Him. Has this happen to you?

"For those who are according to the flesh and are controlled by its unholy desires set their minds on and pursue those things which gratify the flesh, but those who are according to the Spirit and are controlled by the desires of the Spirit set their minds on and seek those things which gratify the [Holy] Spirit. Now the mind of the flesh [which is sense and reason without the Holy Spirit] is death [death that comprises all the miseries arising from sin, both here and hereafter]. But the mind of the [Holy] Spirit is life and [soul] peace [both now and forever]" (Romans 8:5–6 AMPC).

ETERNAL LIFE POINT: Having the mindset of Christ Jesus daily is not optional; it's a requirement—a conscious choice made each and every day!

"So then, brethren, we are debtors, but not to the flesh [we are not obligated to our carnal nature], to live [a life ruled by the standards set up by the dictates] of the flesh. For if you live according to [the dictates of] the flesh, you will surely die. But if through the power of the [Holy] Spirit you are [habitually] putting to death (making extinct, deadening) the [evil] deeds prompted by the body, you shall [really and genuinely] live forever. For all who are led by the Spirit of God are sons of God" (Romans 8:12–14 AMPC).

Every Believer Is to Have the Mind of Christ
"Now we have not received the spirit [that belongs to] the world, but the [Holy] Spirit Who is from God, [given to us] that we might realize and comprehend and appreciate the gifts [of divine favor and blessing so freely and lavishly] bestowed on us by God. And we are setting these truths forth in words not taught by human wisdom but taught by the [Holy] Spirit, combining and interpreting spiritual truths with spiritual language [to those who possess the Holy Spirit]. But the natural, nonspiritual man does not accept or welcome or admit into his heart the gifts and teachings and revelations of the Spirit of God, for they are folly (meaningless nonsense) to him; and he is incapable of knowing them [of progressively recognizing, understanding, and becoming better acquainted with them] because they are spiritually discerned and estimated and appreciated. But the spiritual man tries all things [he examines, investigates, inquiries into, questions, and discerns all things], yet is himself to be put on trial and judged by no one [he can read the meaning of everything, but no one can properly discern or appraise or get an insight into him]. For who has known or understood the mind (the counsels and purposes) of the Lord so as to guide and instruct Him and give Him knowledge? But we have the mind of Christ (the Messiah) and do hold the thoughts (feelings and purposes) of His heart [Isaiah 40:13]" (1 Corinthians 2:12–16 AMPC).

A Choice to Be Made
"Let this same attitude and purpose and [humble] mind be in you which was in Christ Jesus: [Let Him be your example in humility:]" (Philippians 2:5 AMPC).

ETERNAL LIFE POINT: Every believer must make a daily conscious choice of the mindset by which he or she will live.

iii. Living from position and identity creates the empowerment of Jesus Christ by the infilling presence of the Holy Spirit. It is not optional;

it's a requirement to be practiced daily. "Therefore, [there is] now no condemnation (no adjudging guilty of wrong) for those who are in Christ Jesus, who live [and] walk not after the dictates of the flesh, but after the dictates of the Spirit [John 3:18]. For the law of the Spirit of life [which is] in Christ Jesus [the law of our new being] has freed me from the law of sin and of death" (Romans 8:1–2 AMPC). Have you truly experienced this heavenly reality of freedom?

"Your old life is dead. Your new life, which is your real life—even though invisible to spectators—is with Christ in God. He is your life. When Christ (your real life, remember) shows up again on this earth, you'll show up, too—the real you, the glorious you. Meanwhile, be content with obscurity, like Christ" (Colossians 3:3–4 MSG).

How does anyone put themselves to death and live for the sake of Christ? By the empowerment and infilling presence of the Spirit of God. This again is a choice that must be made on a continual and habitual practice of internalizing (acknowledging) the presence of the Holy Spirit in our lives daily.

ETERNAL LIFE POINT: The physical moment of now is the greatest opportunity to give expression to the spiritual presence of now!

"And do not get drunk with wine, for that is debauchery; but ever be filled and stimulated with the [Holy] Spirit [Proverbs 23:20]" (Ephesians 5:18 AMPC).

The scripture declares over our lives these truths:

Christ Is Our Real Life Today
"For [as far as this world is concerned] you have died, and your [new, real] life is hidden with Christ in God. When Christ, who is our life, appears, then you also will appear with Him in [the splendor of His] glory" (Colossians 3:3–4 AMPC).

Copartners in the Divine Nature of God
Our practice of living in this physical moment is our daily practice

of living in the spiritual moment of now. What truly is our spiritual moment of now? This truth is based on 1 John 1–4.

"What was from the beginning, what we have heard, what we have seen with our eyes, what we have looked at and touched with our hands, concerning the Word of Life—and the life was manifested, and we have seen and testify and proclaim to you the eternal life, which was with the Father and was manifested to us—what we have seen and heard we proclaim to you also, so that you too may have fellowship with us; and indeed our fellowship is with the Father, and with His Son Jesus Christ. These things we write, so that our joy may be made complete" (1 John 1:1–4 NASB).

Let's look at these statements: "concerning the Word of Life" and "the eternal life, which was with the Father and was manifested to us." We should understand that these statements are both speaking about and of Jesus Christ. In studying this out, we will learn that Jesus Himself is eternal life. And the word *eternal* means "always present, ageless, and timeless." Putting this together, we can understand that Jesus Christ is the eternal word as well as the eternal life that was with the eternal God Who was from the beginning and is the ending. Therefore, every true believer who is in Christ Jesus is already living in the eternal moment of now. We again are now left with a choice to live in His divine power or the physical moment of the mindset of the flesh.

Our Encouragement for Living in the Divine Power of Now
"For His divine power has bestowed upon us all things that [are requisite and suited] to life and godliness, through the [full, personal] knowledge of Him Who called us by and to His own glory and excellence (virtue). By means of these He has bestowed on us His precious and exceedingly great promises, so that through them you may escape [by flight] from the moral decay (rottenness and corruption) that is in the world because of covetousness (lust and greed), and become sharers (partakers) of the divine nature. For this very reason, adding your diligence [to the divine promises], employ every effort in exercising your faith to develop virtue (excellence, resolution, Christian energy),

and in [exercising] virtue [develop] knowledge (intelligence), and in [exercising] knowledge [develop] self-control, and in [exercising] self-control [develop] steadfastness (patience, endurance), and in [exercising] steadfastness [develop] godliness (piety), and in [exercising] godliness [develop] brotherly affection, and in [exercising] brotherly affection [develop] Christian love. For as these qualities are yours and increasingly abound in you, they will keep [you] from being idle or unfruitful unto the [full personal] knowledge of our Lord Jesus Christ (the Messiah, the anointed One). For whoever lacks these qualities is blind, [spiritually] shortsighted, seeing only what is near to him, and has become oblivious [to the fact] that he was cleansed from his old sins. Because of this, brethren, be all the more solicitous and eager to make sure (to ratify, to strengthen, to make steadfast) your calling and election; for if you do this, you will never stumble or fall. Thus there will be richly and abundantly provided for your entry into the eternal kingdom of our Lord and Savior Jesus Christ" (2 Peter 1:3–11 AMPC).

ETERNAL LIFE POINT: Having the divine empowerment for living and godliness by being a copartner in the divine nature of Christ Jesus, we are now able through our faith of diligence to walk worthy of our calling.

By the Spirit, I Am Identified as a Follower of Christ Jesus

"But you shall receive power (ability, efficiency, and might) when the Holy Spirit has come upon you, and you shall be My witnesses in Jerusalem and all Judea and Samaria and to the ends (the very bounds) of the earth" (Acts 1:8 AMPC).

ETERNAL LIFE POINT: The infilling of the Holy Spirit is a continual and habitual practice that must be exercised on a daily basis.

iv. Understanding that living from our position and identity creates Heaven's realities on earth.

Living in the Eternal Moment of Now
"[We are writing] about the Word of Life [in] Him Who existed from the

beginning, whom we have heard, Whom we have seen with our [own] eyes, Whom we have gazed upon [for ourselves] and have touched with our [own] hands. And the Life [an aspect of His being] was revealed (made manifest, demonstrated), and we saw [as eyewitnesses] and are testifying to and declare to you the Life, the eternal Life [in Him] Who already existed with the Father and Who [actually] was made visible (was revealed) to us [His followers]. What we have seen and [ourselves] heard, we are also telling you, so that you too may realize and enjoy fellowship as partners and partakers with us. And [this] fellowship that we have [which is a distinguishing mark of Christians] is with the Father and with His Son Jesus Christ (the Messiah)" (1 John 1:1–3 AMPC).

ETERNAL LIFE POINT: Christ Jesus, our position and identity, is always present, ageless, and timeless; our eternal victory in the moment of now as believers lives daily from the Kingdom.

The eternal life points and scriptures are for intentional internal focused faith!

When does someone receive this eternal truth? "Now."

"When?" "Now," he said. "Never another time. Never tomorrow. You can only come to Him when the time is now. No other time is real. So the only one who can come is you . . . the only place is here . . . and the only time is now." "And so the voice of God would now call to the one who is here and now and to each one who would hear His voice wherever and whenever they are . . . the voice of God would say to you this . . . I have known you from the beginning, from before you took your first step, before you breathed your first breath, before you were even conceived. I have seen all your tears and have known all your sorrows and wounds and pains, all your longings and hopes, all your fears, your dreams and heartbreaks, your burdens and weariness, your times of asking Me why, your cries of loneliness and emptiness, your times of separation, your mourning for what was lost, your weaknesses and failings, your wanderings, your sins and shame . . . and I have still loved you with an everlasting love . . . and now I call you to leave the darkness and all that is passed and all that I never willed or purposed for your life . . . that the days of your separation would come to an end. It is time now to return. It is time to come home . . . to enter the inheritance of blessing you never knew but were born to enter. It is time for your Jubilee. Come to Me, and I will not turn you away but will receive you. And I will wipe away all your tears. I will forgive all your sins. I will heal all your wounds. And I will turn all your sorrows into joy. And you will forget your days of darkness and wandering, the days of your separation. And I will make all things new. And I will bring you into a land where the crippled walk, where deserts bloom, where the blind see, where the defiled become pure, and where that which was lost is found again. I will bring you to a place you have never known and yet have always longed to be, to your Promised Land. And I will never leave you. And you will never again know what it is to be lost. For in that day, you will have come home. You will be Mine, and I will be yours . . . forever" (prayer by Jonathan Cahn).

Life Application

1. How does this truth encourage you in your daily walk with those around you?
2. What life truth can you apply to your everyday living?
3. What scripture verses would you choose to memorize and why?
4. Write a life application from this teaching.

Concentrate and Meditate on These Words

Dear friends, listen well to my words. Keep my message in plain view at all times. Concentrate! Learn it by heart! Those who discover these words live, really live; body and soul, they're bursting with health. Keep vigilant watch over your heart; that's where life starts. (Proverbs 4:20–23 Message Bible)

God calls us friends; He has five commands:

1. Listen well to His Words.
2. Tune your ears to His voice.
3. Keep His message in plain view at all times.
4. Concentrate on it (intentional internal focused faith).
5. Learn it by heart (memorize it).

Promise to be fulfilled for those who practice these Words: they will live, really live (abundantly), and their bodies and souls will be bursting with health.

Chapter 7

LIVING WITH AND HAVING THE MIND AND HEART OF CHRIST JESUS

(Praying for the Mind of Christ Jesus)

ETERNAL LIFE POINT: Without the mind of Christ Jesus, there can be no Kingdom reality presence.

Growing in the mind of Christ Jesus is the practicing and the perfecting of who we are in the eternal moment of now. This all starts from the moment we arise to the moment we lay our head down for the night. Prayer begins this eternal moment in the morning, and prayer ends the eternal moment.

Practicing Our Morning Prayer for Intentional Internal Focused Faith: Living from Heaven to Earth!

We are made complete in Him!

"Therefore as you have received Christ Jesus the Lord, so walk in

Him, having been firmly rooted and now being built up in Him and established in your faith, just as you were instructed, and overflowing with gratitude. See to it that no one takes you captive through philosophy and empty deception, according to the tradition of men, according to the elementary principles of the world, rather than according to Christ. For in Him all the fullness of Deity dwells in bodily form, and in Him you have been made complete, and He is the head over all rule and authority; and in Him you were also circumcised with a circumcision made without hands, in the removal of the body of the flesh by the circumcision of Christ; having been buried with Him in baptism, in which you were also raised up with Him through faith in the working of God, who raised Him from the dead!" (Colossians 2:6–12 NASB).

Prayer
Heavenly Father, I thank You that I have received Christ Jesus and that I now choose to walk in Him. I am being rooted and built up in Him so that I may be established in my growing faith just as I have been instructed and find myself overflowing with gratitude. Help me to watch over my mind so that I would not be taken captive through philosophies and empty deceptions based on the traditions of men, according to the elementary principles of the world rather than according to Jesus, my Lord.

Father, all the fullness of Deity dwells in Christ Jesus, to which I am made complete. In Jesus I have been circumcised, a circumcision made without hands, as Christ Jesus has removed my body of flesh (sin nature) by His death on the cross for me. I am buried with Him and have been raised to a new life in Him as He sits at the right hand of the Father, so I sit in Him!

We Have the Spirit of God the Father
"For to us God revealed (His wisdom) thoughts through the Spirit; for the Spirit searches all things, even the depths of God. For who among men knows the thoughts of a man except the spirit of the man which is in him? Even so the thoughts of God no one know except the Spirit of God. Now we have received, not the spirit of the world, but the Spirit

who is from God, so that we may know the things freely given to us by God, which things we also speak, not in words taught by human wisdom, but in those taught by the Spirit, combining spiritual thoughts with spiritual words!"

Father, I thank You that You have given to me Your Holy Spirit so that I may know the deep things of Your heart toward me and my circumstances and situations. By Your Spirit, I am able to discern and evaluate and appraise my life circumstances and situations so that I may be able to make Heaven to earth choices that bring glory to Your name, combining spiritual thoughts with spiritual words.

But We Have the Mind of Christ!
"But a natural man does not accept the things of the Spirit of God, for they are foolishness to him; and he cannot understand them, because they are spiritually appraised. But he who is spiritual appraises all things, yet he himself is appraised by no one. FOR WHO HAS KNOWN THE MIND OF THE LORD, THAT HE WILL INSTRUCT HIM? But we have the mind of Christ!" (1 Corinthians 2:10–16 NASB).

Lord, how thankful I am for the mind of Christ Jesus, allowing me to focus on the things above and not on the things of the earth. I thank You that because I have the mind of Christ Jesus, I am able to understand the things of the Spirit and appraise all things!

Focus on the Truth about You!
"Rejoice in the Lord always; again I will say, rejoice! Let your gentle spirit be known to all men. The Lord is near. Be anxious for nothing, but in everything by prayer and supplication with thanksgiving let your requests be made known to God. And the peace of God, which surpasses all comprehension, will guard your hearts and your minds in Christ Jesus. Finally, brethren, whatever is true, whatever is honorable, whatever is right, whatever is pure, whatever is lovely, whatever is of good repute, if there is any excellence and if anything worthy of praise, dwell on these things. The things you have learned and received and

heard and seen in me, practice these things, and the God of peace will be with you!" (Philippians 4:4–9 NASB).

Lord, because I have the mind of Christ Jesus, I am able to rejoice always, for I have a quiet and gentle spirit before all men. Being anxious for nothing but in everything by prayer and supplication with thanksgiving, I am able to let my request be made known to God. For the peace of God is able to surpass all my comprehension, guarding my heart and mind in Christ Jesus. Lord, with Your mind in me, I am able to focus on whatever is true, whatever is honorable, whatever is right, whatever is pure, whatever is lovely, and whatever is of good repute. I am able to dwell upon whatever is excellent and praiseworthy. Because of my dwelling upon the things above, my God of peace will be with me!

We Are Copartner in His Divine Nature

"Seeing that His divine power has granted to us everything pertaining to life and godliness, through the true knowledge of Him who called us by His own glory and excellence. For by these He has granted to us His precious and magnificent promises, so that by them you may become partakers of the divine nature, having escaped the corruption that is in the world by lust. Now for this very reason also, applying all diligence, in your faith supply moral excellence, and in your moral excellence, knowledge, and in your knowledge, self-control, and in your self-control, perseverance, and in your perseverance, godliness, and in your godliness, brotherly kindness, and in your brotherly kindness, love. For if these qualities are yours and are increasing, they render you neither useless nor unfruitful in the true knowledge of our Lord Jesus Christ. For he who lacks these qualities is blind or short-sighted, having forgotten his purification from his former sins. Therefore, brethren, be all the more diligent to make certain about His calling and choosing you; for as long as you practice these things, you will never stumble; for in this way the entrance into the eternal kingdom of our Lord and Savior Jesus Christ will be abundantly supplied to you" (2 Peter 1:3–11 NASB).

Lord God, thank You that You have given to me everything pertaining to life and godliness as I grow in the true knowledge of my Lord and

Savior, Who has called me by His own glory and excellence. Lord, You have by Your precious and magnificent promises made me a copartner of your divine nature so that I can escape the corruption that is in the world around me and of my own lustful flesh. Lord Jesus, by the enabling empowerment of the Spirit, I can practice with all diligence in my faith, moral excellence, knowledge, self-control, perseverance, godliness, brotherly kindness, and love.

Lord, by dwelling on these character traits, I will not be blind or shortsighted but found useful and fruitful in all I do. Father God, thank You that as I practice these qualities I will never stumble or fall, but the way into the Eternal Kingdom by my Lord and Savior, Jesus Christ, will be abundantly supplied to me!

Setting My Mind on the Things Above!
"Therefore if you have been raised up with Christ, keep seeking the things above, where Christ is, seated at the right hand of God. Set your mind on the things above, not on the things that are on earth. For you have died and your life is hidden with Christ in God. When Christ, who is our life, is revealed, then you also will be revealed with Him in glory" (Colossians 3:1–4 NASB).

Father God, because You have raised me up with Christ Jesus, I will practice seeking the things above. For I am dead, hidden in Christ Jesus in You, Father God. Now Jesus is my real life, and I choose to remain in Him until He returns for me, knowing at His return, I then can be seen, as His glory will be all around me!

Father God, You have called and purposed for me to follow after the example of my Lord and Savior, Jesus Christ, Who committed no sin, nor was any deceit found in His mouth. While He was being reviled, He did not revile in return; while suffering, He uttered no threats but kept entrusting Himself to You, Father God.

Lord Jesus, let this be a truthful practice of my life for You today in behalf of all who come near me today. For by Your wounds I am healed. Lord, I therefore arm myself to suffer for the sake of Christ Jesus in behalf of others so that they may experience Your heavenly realities for themselves today. For I live for Your will, Father God, to be done on earth as it is in Heaven. Amen and amen!

Following My Example (Jesus Christ)!
"For you have been called for this purpose, since Christ also suffered for you, leaving you an example for you to follow in His steps, WHO COMMITTED NO SIN, NOR WAS ANY DECEIT FOUND IN HIS MOUTH; and while being reviled, He did not revile in return; while suffering, He uttered no threats, but kept entrusting Himself to Him who judges righteously; and He Himself bore our sins in His body on the cross, so that we might die to sin and live to righteousness; for by His wounds you were healed" (1 Peter 2:21–24 NASB).

"Therefore, since Christ has suffered in the flesh, arm yourselves also with the same purpose, because he who has suffered in the flesh has ceased from sin, so as to live the rest of the time in the flesh no longer for the lusts of men, but for the will of God" (1 Peter 4:1–2 NASB).

Living from Heaven to Earth!

My dear friends, brothers, and sisters in our Lord and Savior, Jesus Christ, this is what it means by putting on the Lord Jesus Christ and walking in a manner that is worthy of your calling. Be encouraged and unafraid in your growing of the truth that already resides in you. My heart would be that we take these verses and the prayers, follow them, and memorize them all until they become the full expression of our everyday living.

Life Application

1. From our scriptures and prayers in this chapter, what caught your attention?
2. Set aside time to rememorize the verses and prayers for the renewing of your mind.
3. What life application do you take from this chapter, and how can you put it into a life walk worthy of your calling?

Concentrate and Meditate on These Words

Dear friends, listen well to my words. Keep my message in plain view at all times. Concentrate! Learn it by heart! Those who discover these words live, really live; body and soul, they're bursting with health. Keep vigilant watch over your heart; that's where life starts. (Proverbs 4:20–23 Message Bible)

God calls us friends; He has five commands:

1. Listen well to His Words.
2. Tune your ears to His voice.
3. Keep His message in plain view at all times.
4. Concentrate on it (intentional internal focused faith).
5. Learn it by heart (memorize it).

Promise to be fulfilled for those who practice these Words: they will live, really live (abundantly), and their bodies and souls will be bursting with health.

Chapter 8

LIVING BY THE LIFE OF THE SPIRIT

ETERNAL LIFE POINT: Living by the life of the Holy Spirit is the only way to be identified as a son or daughter of God.

"So then, brethren, we are under obligation, not to the flesh, to live according to the flesh—for if you are living according to the flesh, you must die; but if by the Spirit you are putting to death the deeds of the body, you will live. For all who are being led by the Spirit of God, these are sons of God" (Romans 8:12–14 NASB).

The Life and Light of Obedience

ETERNAL LIFE POINT: Walking in the life and light of obedience is not optional; it's a choice of/to full obedience!

God's purpose: The life and light of obedience in the life of every believer creates thoughts and attitudes that produce words and behaviors that display the Kingdom's realities in all they do.

"For I will take you from among the nations and gather you out of all countries and bring you into your own land. Then will I sprinkle clean water upon you, and you shall be clean from all your uncleanness; and from all your idols will I cleanse you. A new heart will I give you and a new spirit will I put within you, and I will take away the stony heart out of your flesh and give you a heart of flesh. And I will put my Spirit within you and cause you to walk in My statutes, and you shall heed My ordinances and do them" (Ezekiel 36:24–27 AMPC).

Spirit of Obedience Is in Every Believer
"Then I will sprinkle clean water on you, and you will be clean. Your filth will be washed away, and you will no longer worship idols. And I will give you a new heart, and I will put a new spirit in you. I will take out your stony, stubborn heart and give you a tender, responsive heart. And I will put my Spirit in you so that you will follow my decrees and be careful to obey my regulations" (Ezekiel 36:25–27 NLT).

"But when God found fault with the people, he said: 'The day is coming, says the Lord, when I will make a new covenant with the people of Israel and Judah. This covenant will not be like the one I made with their ancestors when I took them by the hand and led them out of the land of Egypt. They did not remain faithful to my covenant, so I turned my back on them, says the Lord. But this is the new covenant I will make with the people of Israel on that day, says the Lord: I will put my laws in their minds, and I will write them on their hearts. I will be their God, and they will be my people" (Hebrews 8:8–10 NLT).

ETERNAL LIFE POINT: Every born-again believer who has received a new heart and new spirit becomes the reflection of the image of Christ Jesus, whose obedience now produces Heaven's realities to the world in which he or she lives.

Jesus Christ, Our Reflection (Two Reflections to Focus On)
"Don't believe Me unless I carry out My Father's work" (John 10:37 NLT).

"For this purpose, the Son of God was manifested, that He might destroy the works of the devil" (1 John 3: 8).

For hundreds of years, the prophets spoke of the Messiah's coming. They gave over three hundred specific details describing Him. Jesus fulfilled them all!

The angels also gave witness to His divinity when they came with a message for the shepherds: "For there is born to you this day . . . a Savior, who is Christ the Lord" (Luke 2: 11).

Nature itself testified to the arrival of the Messiah with the star that led the wise men (see Matthew 2:1). Yet with this one statement, "Unless I do the works of the Father, do not believe Me" (John 10: 37), Jesus put the credibility of all these messengers on the line. Their ministries would have been in vain without one more ingredient to confirm who He really was. That ingredient was miracles (signs and wonders).

Paul Declares Signs and Wonders

"As for myself, brethren, when I came to you, I did not come proclaiming to you the testimony and evidence or mystery and secret of God [concerning what He has done through Christ for the salvation of men] in lofty words of eloquence or human philosophy and wisdom; For I resolved to know nothing (to be acquainted with nothing, to make a display of the knowledge of nothing, and to be conscious of nothing) among you except Jesus Christ (the Messiah) and Him crucified. And I was in (passed into a state of) weakness and fear (dread) and great trembling [after I had come] among you. And my language and my message were not set forth in persuasive (enticing and plausible) words of wisdom, but they were in demonstration of the [Holy] Spirit and power [a proof by the Spirit and power of God, operating on me and stirring in the minds of my hearers the most holy emotions and thus persuading them], so that your faith might not rest in the wisdom of men (human philosophy), but in the power of God" (1 Corinthians 2:1–5 AMPC).

Let each and every one understand that Jesus gave every individual the right to disbelieve it all if there was no demonstration of power upon His ministry.

Every believer who is a true follower of Jesus Christ should hunger for the day when the church will make the same statement to the world. If we're not doing the miracles that Jesus did, you don't have to believe us.

Even as a Child, Jesus Knew His Assignment
The verses mentioned here deal with two subjects—doing the works of the Father and destroying the works of the devil. These two things are inseparable. They help to clarify the purpose for Christ's coming. He was driven by one overwhelming passion: pleasing His Heavenly Father. The unveiling of His priorities started long before His ministry began. He was only twelve. The realization that Jesus was missing came after Mary and Joseph had traveled several days from Jerusalem. They returned to search for their twelve-year-old son.

We can only imagine what might have been going through their minds during their three days of separation. He was their miracle child . . . the Promised One. Did they lose Him through carelessness? Was their job of raising Him finished? Had they failed?

They finally found Him in the temple discussing the scriptures with adults! There's no doubt they were very happy and relieved. But realistically, they were probably also a bit upset.

To make matters worse, Jesus didn't seem the least bit concerned about their anxiety. In fact, He seemed a little surprised that they didn't know where He'd be. We hear no apology; we find no explanations, just a statement about His priorities: "Did you not know that I must be about My Father's business?" (Luke 2:49). Here the revelation of purpose began.

The first and only recorded words of Jesus in His youth were all about His purpose. Obeying the Father was His whole ambition. As He got older, He confessed that obeying the Father remained His priority. It actually brought Him nourishment—"My food is to do the will of Him who sent Me" (John 4:34).

Eighteen years later, at the beginning of His ministry, Jesus is found teaching His disciples what He tried to teach Mom and Dad: the priority of the Father's business.

Statements such as "I can of Myself do nothing" (John 5: 19), "I do not seek My own will but the will of the Father" (John 5: 30), and "I always do those things that please Him" (John 8: 29) all testify of His utter dependence on the Father and His one passion to please Him alone.

"Jesus said, 'I tell you the truth, Moses didn't give you bread from heaven. My Father did. And now he offers you the true bread from heaven. The true bread of God is the one who comes down from heaven and gives life to the world.' 'Sir,' they said, 'give us that bread every day.' Jesus replied, 'I am the bread of life. Whoever comes to me will never be hungry again. Whoever believes in me will never be thirsty. However, those the Father has given me will come to me, and I will never reject them. For I have come down from heaven to do the will of God who sent me, not to do my own will. And this is the will of God, that I should not lose even one of all those he has given me, but that I should raise them up at the last day. For it is my Father's will that all who see his Son and believe in him should have eternal life. I will raise them up at the last day'" (John 6:32–35, 37–40 NLT).

The secret of His ministry is seen in His statements: "The Son can do nothing of Himself, but what He sees the Father do . . . the Son also does in like manner" (John 5: 19) and "I speak to the world those things which I heard from Him" (John 8: 26).

His obedience put the bounty of Heaven on a collision course with the desperate condition of mankind on earth. It was His dependence on the Father that brought forth the reality of the Kingdom into this world. It's what enabled Him to say, "The Kingdom of Heaven is at hand!" (Some thought taken from Bill Johnson's book *When Heaven Invades Earth.*)

It is this to which you and I have been purposed and called; the apostle Peter says it like this:

"For even to this were you called [it is inseparable from your vocation]. For Christ also suffered for you, leaving you [His personal] example, so that you should follow in His footsteps" (1 Peter 2:21 AMPC).

"So, since Christ suffered in the flesh for us, for you, arm yourselves with the same thought and purpose [patiently to suffer rather than fail to please God]. For whoever has suffered in the flesh [having the mind of Christ] is done with [intentional] sin [has stopped pleasing himself and the world, and pleases God], so that he can no longer spend the rest of his natural life living by [his] human appetites and desires, but [he lives] for what God wills" (1 Peter 4:1–2 AMPC).

The Life and Light of Obedience Produces Heaven's Realities

"But I say, walk and live [habitually] in the [Holy] Spirit [responsive to and controlled and guided by the Spirit]; then you will certainly not gratify the cravings and desires of the flesh (of human nature without God)."

ETERNAL LIFE POINT: The life and light of obedience produces the fruit of the Holy Spirit, the true evidence of the Kingdom's realities.

"But the fruit of the [Holy] Spirit [the work which His presence within accomplishes] is love, joy (gladness), peace, patience (an even temper, forbearance), kindness, goodness (benevolence), faithfulness, Gentleness (meekness, humility), self-control (self-restraint, continence). Against such things there is no law [that can bring a charge]. And those who belong to Christ Jesus (the Messiah) have crucified the flesh (the godless human nature) with its passions and appetites and desires. If we live by the [Holy] Spirit, let us also walk by the Spirit. [If by the Holy Spirit we have our life in God, let us go forward walking in line, our conduct controlled by the Spirit.]" (Galatians 5:16, 22–25 AMPC).

Here again it sounds like we have a choice to make; if by the Holy Spirit we have our life in God, let us go forward walking in line, our conduct controlled by the Spirit.

The choice is yours to make!

Life Application

1. What's your understanding of the word *obedience* from this teaching?
2. What truth do you need to practice from this teaching?
3. What's a life application you can take from this teaching?
4. Write a prayer for yourself from this teaching.

Concentrate and Meditate on These Words

Dear friends, listen well to my words. Keep my message in plain view at all times. Concentrate! Learn it by heart! Those who discover these words live, really live; body and soul, they're bursting with health. Keep vigilant watch over your heart; that's where life starts. (Proverbs 4:20–23 Message Bible).

God calls us friends; He has five commands:

1. Listen well to His Words.
2. Tune your ears to His voice.
3. Keep His message in plain view at all times.
4. Concentrate on it (intentional internal focused faith).
5. Learn it by heart (memorize it).

Promise to be fulfilled for those who practice these Words: they will live, really live (abundantly), and their bodies and souls will be bursting with health.

Chapter 9

WALKING LIKE WE'RE THE
LIGHT OF THE WORLD

Therefore, my dear people, run away from idolatry.
—1 Corinthians 10:14 Kingdom New Testament

Whatever you love the most directs what you think, say, and do.
—Romans 1:1–32 AMPC

In my book *Dying to Live in the Eternal Moment of Now*, I shared that we have four things in life to control. Everything starts with our thoughts. Our thoughts create our attitudes, our attitudes create words focused upon and spoken, then our spoken words create actions and behaviors. Life behaviors create life patterns.

Sin—that is, a toxic mindset or worldview—starts with a thought. We focus our attention on something, thinking about it daily, giving it power and strength in the substrates of our brain through the quantum signals we send. We essentially make it our idol; our attention is worship. In the writings of the apostle Paul, sin begins with idolatry.

We don't just do something bad out of the blue. Wrongdoing always starts in the mind, and as we think about it, allowing it to shape what we say and do, we trade in the image of God for an idol, whether it is bitterness, jealousy, power, sex, money, or anything other than God, Who is love. We become what we think about the most, so we need to constantly be aware of what we are thinking. If you have a toxic pattern that is manifesting in your life, this means you have dedicated time to growing it over sixty-three-plus days—the time it takes to build a good, or a bad, habit (Dr. Caroline Leaf, *Switch On Your Brain*).

This is why Jesus Christ came into the world—so that He might deliver humanity from the darkness of their minds.

It is only the life and light of obedience (Jesus Christ) that produces the Kingdom's realities in the life of every believer.

Jesus Spoke of the Importance of Seeing and Hearing
"Then when they were alone, he turned to the disciples and said, 'Blessed are the eyes that see what you have seen. I tell you, many prophets and kings longed to see what you see, but they didn't see it. And they longed to hear what you hear, but they didn't hear it'" (Luke 10:23–24 NLT).

"Then he said, 'When I was with you before, I told you that everything written about me in the law of Moses and the prophets and in the Psalms must be fulfilled.' Then he opened their minds to understand the Scriptures" (Luke 24:45 NLT).

Is there a seeing and hearing problem with humanity?

"So this I say, and affirm together with the Lord, that you walk no longer just as the Gentiles also walk, in the futility of their mind, being darkened in their understanding, excluded from the life of God because of the ignorance that is in them, because of the hardness of their heart; and they, having become callous, have given themselves over to sensuality for the practice of every kind of impurity with greediness. But you did not learn Christ in this way, if indeed you have heard Him and have been taught in Him, just as truth is in Jesus, that, in reference to your former manner of life, you lay aside the old self, which is being corrupted in accordance with the lusts of deceit, and that you be renewed in the spirit of your mind, and put on the new self, which in the likeness of God has been created in righteousness and holiness of the truth" (Ephesians 4:17–24 NASB).

ETERNAL LIFE POINT: Without open eyes through a relationship with Jesus Christ, there can be no revelation to spiritual truth. Walking in the light of truth is a choice that is empowered by the living presence of the Holy Spirit.

ETERNAL LIFE POINT: Where we refuse to be the light, we give darkness permission to rule over our present moment (we are the light of the Kingdom's presence). When we refuse to be the light, we are thinking with the mindset of the flesh, not the mindset of the Spirit (Romans 8:5–6 NASB).

"Those who are dominated by the sinful nature think about sinful things, but those who are controlled by the Holy Spirit think about things that please the Spirit. So letting your sinful nature control your mind leads to death. But letting the Spirit control your mind leads to life and peace" (Romans 8:5–6 NLT).

ETERNAL LIFE POINT: Every believer is to be the evidence of the Kingdom's life and peace; as the life and light of Christ Jesus shines through them by the Holy Spirit's empowerment in every aspect of their being, Heaven's realities then find expression here on earth.

Jesus, the Light of the World
"In the beginning the Word already existed. The Word was with God, and the Word was God. He existed in the beginning with God. God created everything through him, and nothing was created except through him. The Word gave life to everything that was created, and his life brought light to everyone. The light shines in the darkness, and the darkness can never extinguish it" (John 1:1–5 NLT).

"In the beginning [before all time] was the Word (Christ), and the

Word was with God, and the Word was God Himself [Isaiah 9:6]. He was present originally with God. All things were made and came into existence through Him; and without Him was not even one thing made that has come into being. In Him was Life, and the Life was the Light of men. And the Light shines on in the darkness, for the darkness has never overpowered it [put it out or absorbed it or appropriated it, and is unreceptive to it]. There came a man sent from God, whose name was John [Malachi 3:1]. This man came to witness, that he might testify of the Light, that all men might believe in it [adhere to it, trust it, and rely upon it] through him. He was not the Light himself, but came that he might bear witness regarding the Light. There it was—the true Light [was then] coming into the world [the genuine, perfect, steadfast Light] that illumines every person [Isaiah 49:6]" (John 1:1–9 AMPC).

ETERNAL LIFE POINT: The extinguishing of the Kingdom's light is a choice made by each individual believer.

God's purpose: To show "you are the light of the world—like a city on a hilltop that cannot be hidden. No one lights a lamp and then puts it under a basket. Instead, a lamp is placed on a stand, where it gives light to everyone in the house. In the same way, let your good deeds shine out for all to see, so that everyone will praise your heavenly Father" (Matthew 5:14–16 NLT).

ETERNAL LIFE POINT: Our good deeds that flow from our position and our identity in Christ Jesus become the life and light to the world, which becomes the evidence that the Kingdom is in our midst.

Fulfilling Our Purpose
"Go and announce to them that the Kingdom of Heaven is near. Heal the sick, raise the dead, cure those with leprosy, and cast out demons. Give as freely as you have received!" (Matthew 10:7–8 NLT).

"This is the message we have heard from Him and announce to you, that God is Light, and in Him there is no darkness at all. If we say that we have fellowship with Him and yet walk in the darkness, we lie and do not practice the truth; but if we walk in the Light as He Himself is in the Light, we have fellowship with one another, and the blood of Jesus His Son cleanses us from all sin" (1 John 1:5–7 NASB).

Walking in the light is not optional; it's who we are in Christ Jesus, Who is the life and light of the world.

Why Our Sun Exists

The *sun* is the source of all energy, heat, and light. The amount of sunlight in an area determines what *living thing* can survive there. All plants use sunlight to make food (sugars) in a process called photosynthesis. They store the food in their leaves, and the energy flows to other animals that eat the leaves.

Nothing is more important to us on earth than the sun. Without the sun's heat and light, the earth would be a lifeless ball of ice-coated rock. The sun warms our seas, stirs our atmosphere, generates our weather patterns, and gives energy to the growing green plants that provide the food and oxygen for life on earth.

"In the beginning God created the heavens and the earth. The earth was formless and void, and darkness was over the surface of the deep, and the Spirit of God was moving over the surface of the waters. Then God said, 'Let there be light'; and there was light. God saw that the light was good; and God separated the light from the darkness. God called the light day, and the darkness He called night. And there was evening and there was morning, one day" (Genesis 1:1–5 NASB).

Why the Son Exists

"In the beginning was the Word, and the Word was with God, and the Word was God. He was in the beginning with God. All things came into being through Him, and apart from Him nothing came into being that has come into being. The Light shines in the darkness, and the darkness did not comprehend it. There came a man sent from God, whose name was John. He came as a witness, to testify about the Light, so that all might believe through him. He was not the Light, but he came to testify about the Light.

"The Word gave life to everything that was created, and his life brought light to everyone. The light shines in the darkness, and the darkness can never extinguish it. God sent a man, John the Baptist, to tell about the light so that everyone might believe because of his testimony. John himself was not the light; he was simply a witness to tell about the light. The one who is the true light, who gives light to everyone, was coming into the world. He came into the very world he created, but the world didn't recognize him. He came to his own people, and even they rejected him. But to all who believed him and accepted him, he gave the right to become children of God" (John 1:4–12 NLT).

"For he has rescued us from the kingdom of darkness and transferred us into the Kingdom of his dear Son (Life and Light), who purchased our freedom and forgave our sins" (Colossians 1:13–14 NLT).

ETERNAL LIFE POINT: The eternal light and life in every believer creates and produces the Kingdom's realities from a heart of obedience.

Walking in the light and life of obedience is the path that each believer must choose as they follow the example of Christ Jesus.

"For you have been called for this purpose, since Christ also suffered for you, leaving you an example for you to follow in His steps" (1 Peter 2:21 NASB).

The life and light of obedience in the life of every believer creates thoughts and attitudes that produce words and behaviors that display the Kingdom's realities in all they do.

Walking in the life and light is not optional; it's a choice of full obedience! We are encouraged to captive every thought to the obedience of Christ.

"For though we walk in the flesh [as mortal men], we are not carrying on our [spiritual] warfare according to the flesh and using the weapons of man. The weapons of our warfare are not physical [weapons of flesh and blood]. Our weapons are divinely powerful for the destruction of fortresses. We are destroying sophisticated arguments and every exalted and proud thing that sets itself up against the [true] knowledge of God, and we are taking every thought and purpose captive to the obedience of Christ" (2 Corinthians 10:3–5 AMP).

Life Application

1. Do those around you see the life and light of Christ Jesus in everything you say and do?
2. What scripture verse stands out to you and why?
3. Memorize those verses of scripture that will change your life to full obedience.
4. What's your life application from this teaching?

Concentrate and Meditate on These Words

Dear friends, listen well to my words. Keep my message in plain view at all times. Concentrate! Learn it by heart! Those who discover these words live, really live; body and soul, they're bursting with health. Keep vigilant watch over your heart; that's where life starts. (Proverbs 4:20–23 Message Bible)

God calls us friends; He has five commands:

1. Listen well to His Words.
2. Tune your ears to His voice.
3. Keep His message in plain view at all times.
4. Concentrate on it (intentional internal focused faith).
5. Learn it by heart (memorize it).

Promise to be fulfilled for those who practice these Words: they will live, really live (abundantly), and their bodies and souls will be bursting with health.

Chapter 10

RESTORING A FALLEN BROTHER

(Burden Bearing Is Not for Sissies)

ETERNAL LIFE POINT: Your empowerment by the Holy Spirit is not in and of itself for you alone!

"The kingdom of God is not a matter of talk but of power" (1 Corinthians 4:20 NIV).

Does your life speak of a very presence power that is beyond your skills and ability?

There Is No Freedom When Consumed by One
Another
"For you were called to freedom, brethren; only do not turn your freedom into an opportunity for the flesh, but through love serve one another. For the whole Law is fulfilled in one word, in the statement, 'YOU SHALL LOVE YOUR NEIGHBOR AS YOURSELF.' But if

you bite and devour one another, take care that you are not consumed by one another" (Galatians 5:13–15 NASB).

How much of our lives are lived for ourselves and ourselves alone? This is a real challenge for each and every one of us. I will never forget the morning that Lord brought this to my attention. I was in a quiet time with the Lord when the Holy Spirit spoke and challenged this area of my life; I was studying the book of Philippians. Listen to these words:

Do nothing from selfishness or empty conceit [through factional motives, or strife], but with [an attitude of] humility [being neither arrogant nor self-righteous], regard others as more important than yourselves. Do not merely look out for your own personal interests, but also for the interests of others. (Philippians 2:3–4 AMP)

When the Spirit brought these words to my attention, I cried out, "Lord, who do you know that does this stuff? Everybody I know has some type of motive behind what they do for others, even those serving in the church. Just watch them when something doesn't go their way." Then I asked the Spirit, "How does anyone do this without some personal motive?" Okay, I said, "How does one do this?" The Spirit said read the next verse:

Have this same attitude in yourselves which was in Christ Jesus [look to Him as your example in selfless humility], who, although He existed in the form and unchanging essence of God [as One with Him, possessing the fullness of all the divine attributes—the entire nature of deity], did not regard equality with God a thing to be grasped or asserted [as if He did not already possess it, or was afraid of losing it]; but emptied Himself [without renouncing or diminishing His deity, but only temporarily giving up the outward expression of divine equality and His rightful dignity] by assuming the form of a bond-servant, and being made in the likeness of men [He became completely human but was without sin, being fully God and fully man]. (Philippians 2:5–7 AMP)

Our empowerment to be like Christ comes to be expressed in relationships, but most Christians do not live their lives with the empowerment of the Holy Spirit in their relationships to those in or around them. We live our lives very selfishly, based on the satisfaction of our self-serving lifestyle. If we meet the needs of others, it is often from an unspoken self-centered motive to be fulfilled in ourselves, because those whom we were serving acted the way we wanted them to.

Death to self is an acknowledged expression heard and even spoken by many believers but not often a lived-out experience in the life of most believers. We are told in Romans 8:12 that we are no longer under obligation to live according to the deeds of the flesh, for if we are living according to the flesh, we must die. But if we are putting the deeds of the flesh to death, we will live by the life of the Spirit.

Most believers will say, "I am only human, and this is who I am," failing to understand that Christ took your flesh nature to the cross, setting every believer free from the crying attitudes of the flesh. We fail to understand that we live from the mindset of the Holy Spirit, not the mindset of the flesh. This is the daily choice of taking our cross and following after Jesus Christ (Luke 9:23–24).

ETERNAL LIFE POINT: Grace is an empowerment that flows as a reflection from the transformed heart that is fully submitted to the full control of a Holy Spirit–led life.

ETERNAL LIFE POINT: The motive and encouragement of grace is a fully lived life in freedom.

"Seek first the kingdom of God" (Matthew 6:33).

Our faith has its anchor in the unseen realm. We as the sons and daughters of God live from the invisible toward the visible. Our faith actualizes what it realizes in the unseen realm. The scriptures contrast the life of faith with the limitations of natural sight. Our faith provides eyes for our hearts to see the true reality of the spiritual world around us.

ETERNAL LIFE POINT: Position creates being, and being establishes the creative flow of fruit bearing. Fruit bearing is a natural process, flowing from the vine into its branches. The fruit bearing of the branches is created by the branch remaining attached or abiding in the vine.

"Brethren, if any person is overtaken in misconduct or sin of any sort, you who are spiritual [who are responsive to and controlled by the Spirit] should set him right and restore and reinstate him, without any sense of superiority and with all gentleness, keeping an attentive eye on yourself, lest you should be tempted also. Bear (endure, carry) one another's burdens and troublesome moral faults, and in this way fulfill and observe perfectly the law of Christ (the Messiah) and complete what is lacking [in your obedience to it]. For if any person thinks himself to be somebody [too important to condescend to shoulder another's load] when he is nobody [of superiority except in his own estimation], he deceives and deludes and cheats himself. But let every person carefully scrutinize and examine and test his own conduct and his own work. He can then have the personal satisfaction and joy of doing something commendable [in itself alone] without [resorting to] boastful comparison with his neighbor. For every person will have to bear (be equal to understanding and calmly receive) his own [little] load [of oppressive faults]" (Galatians 6:1–5 AMPC).

What mindset do you give more attention to when living life with the people in and around your life on a daily basis? Are you listening more to the fleshly being you believe yourself to be, or are you with intentional internal focused faith listening to the voice of the Holy Spirit declaring your being in Christ Jesus?

"People whose lives are determined by human flesh focus their minds on matters to do with the flesh, but people whose lives are determined by the spirit, focus their minds on matters to do with the spirit" (Romans 8:5).

"For those who are according to the flesh and are controlled by its unholy desires set their minds on and pursue those things which gratify the flesh; but those who are according to the Spirit and are controlled by the desires of the Spirit set their minds on and seek those things which gratify the [Holy] Spirit" (Romans 8:5 AMPC).

There are two types of gratification spoken of here: one is the gratification of the flesh, and the other is the gratification of the Holy Spirit.

Both represent a lifestyle of living and responding to those in our lives as well as those around our lives.

The Holy Spirit doesn't force us to listen to Him. As we have stated, we have to choose on a daily basis to let Him (Holy Spirit) help us and guide us. We have to choose to focus our minds on what He is saying, the "matters to do with the Spirit," seeing the world through God's loving eyes. Love demands great freedom; choice gives us that freedom, yet choice has inescapable consequences.

Remember, whatever we think or dwell upon the most grows and determines the course of our thoughts, words, and actions—the course of our lives. When we choose with our minds to listen to and follow the Holy Spirit, our lives change for the better as we learn to become more and more like our Lord and Savior, reflecting God's glory into the world all around us. With the freedom of love comes great responsibility to choose well, which is why we need to listen to the Spirit of God.

ETERNAL LIFE POINT: The presence of the Holy Spirit creates a natural flow of the love of God in the heart of every true believer. The natural flow of freedom comes by one's choice to be renewed in the Spirit of one's mind expressing God's unconditional love in a nonloving circumstance or situation, which gives evidence to who and what controls one's heart.

God's purpose: To show that each empowerment-filled believer is to become the full reflection of a Spirit-led life, reflecting the full image of the unconditional, undeserved love of God as their relationship is fully restored while drawing others back to their rightful place with the Heavenly Father (their Heavenly Creator).

Living Out and Giving Out Undeserved Love

Brethren, if any person is overtaken in misconduct or sin of any sort,

you who are spiritual [who are responsive to and controlled by the
Spirit] should set him right and restore and reinstate him, without any
sense of superiority and with all gentleness, keeping an attentive eye
on yourself, lest you should be tempted also. Bear (endure, carry) one
another's burdens and troublesome moral faults, and in this way fulfill
and observe perfectly the law of Christ (the Messiah) and complete what
is lacking [in your obedience to it]. For if any person thinks himself to
be somebody [too important to condescend to shoulder another's load]
when he is nobody [of superiority except in his own estimation], he
deceives and deludes and cheats himself. (Galatians 6:1–3)

How to Identify Unfailing Love
Therefore if there is any encouragement in Christ, if there is any
consolation of love, if there is any fellowship of the Spirit, if any affection
and compassion, make my joy complete by being of the same mind,
maintaining the same love, united in spirit, intent on one purpose. Do
nothing from selfishness or empty conceit, but with humility of mind
regard one another as more important than yourselves; do not merely
look out for your own personal interests, but also for the interests of
others. (Philippians 2:1–4 NASB)

Acts of Selflessness
For one is regarded favorably (is approved, acceptable, and thankworthy)
if, as in the sight of God, he endures the pain of unjust suffering. [After
all] what kind of glory [is there in it] if, when you do wrong and are
punished for it, you take it patiently? But if you bear patiently with
suffering [which results] when you do right and that is undeserved, it is
acceptable and pleasing to God. For even to this were you called [it is
inseparable from your vocation]. For Christ also suffered for you, leaving
you [His personal] example, so that you should follow in His footsteps.
He was guilty of no sin, neither was deceit (guile) ever found on His lips
[Isaiah 53:9]. When He was reviled and insulted, He did not revile or
offer insult in return; [when] He was abused and suffered, He made
no threats [of vengeance]; but he trusted [Himself and everything] to
Him Who judges fairly. He personally bore our sins in His [own] body
on the tree [as on an altar and offered Himself on it], that we might die

(cease to exist) to sin and live to righteousness. By His wounds you have been healed. For you were going astray like [so many] sheep, but now you have come back to the Shepherd and Guardian (the Bishop) of your souls [Isaiah 53:5, 6]. (1 Peter 2:19-25 AMPC)

Walking by the Spirit
[My] brethren, if anyone among you strays from the truth and falls into error and another [person] brings him back [to God], Let the [latter] one be sure that whoever turns a sinner from his evil course will save [that one's] soul from death and will cover a multitude of sins [procure the pardon of the many sins committed by the convert]. (James 5:19–20 AMPC)

The Daily Arming of the Flesh for Suffering for the Sake of Christ:
Therefore, since Christ has suffered in the flesh, arm yourselves also with the same purpose, because he who has suffered in the flesh has ceased from sin, so as to live the rest of the time in the flesh no longer for the lusts of men, but for the will of God. For the time already past is sufficient for you to have carried out the desire of the Gentiles, having pursued a course of sensuality, lusts, drunkenness, carousing, drinking parties and abominable idolatries. In all this, they are surprised that you do not run with them into the same excesses of dissipation, and they malign you; but they will give account to Him who is ready to judge the living and the dead. For the gospel has for this purpose been preached even to those who are dead, that though they are judged in the flesh as men, they may live in the spirit according to the will of God. The end of all things is near; therefore, be of sound judgment and sober spirit for the purpose of prayer. Above all, keep fervent in your love for one another, because love covers a multitude of sins. (1 Peter 4:1–8 NASB)

It is time for the church to stand up and fight for her brothers and sisters, leading them back to a restored relationship to the Body of Christ and a full restoration to their Heavenly Father.

My brothers and sisters, if anyone among you strays from the truth and falls into error and [another] one turns him back [to God], let the [latter] one know that the one who has turned a sinner from the error of his way will save that one's soul from death (spiritual separation) and cover a multitude of sins [that is, obtain the pardon of the many sins committed by the one who has been restored]. (James 5:19–20 AMP)

Let's start being the church! Life Application

1. Where do you see yourself in this chapter in restoring a fallen brother?
2. What stands out to you that you may need to commit to daily practice?
3. Write out a life application for your daily walk.
4. Write out a prayer that you can walk in daily.

Concentrate and Meditate on These Words

Dear friends, listen well to my words. Keep my message in plain view at all times. Concentrate! Learn it by heart! Those who discover these words live, really live; body and soul, they're bursting with health. Keep vigilant watch over your heart; that's where life starts. (Proverbs 4:20–23 Message Bible)

God calls us friends; He has five commands:

1. Listen well to His Words.
2. Tune your ears to His voice.
3. Keep His message in plain view at all times.
4. Concentrate on it (intentional internal focused faith).
5. Learn it by heart (memorize it).

Promise to be fulfilled for those who practice these Words: they will live, really live (abundantly), and their bodies and souls will be bursting with health.

Chapter 11

TWO EQUAL ONE

Know, Knowledge

The Old Testament. The Hebrew root *yada*, translated "know/ knowledge," appears almost 950 times in the Hebrew Bible. It has a wider sweep than our English word *know*, including *perceiving*, *learning*, *understanding*, *willing*, *performing*, and *experiencing*. To know is not to be intellectually informed about some abstract principle but to apprehend and experience reality. Knowledge is not the possession of information but rather its exercise or actualization.

Thus, to know God biblically is not to know about Him in an abstract and impersonal manner but rather to enter into His saving actions (Micah 6:5). To know God is not to struggle philosophically with His eternal essence but rather to recognize and accept His claims. It is not some mystical contemplation but dutiful obedience.

Three Words that Explain *Know* and *Knowledge*

Simply put, these gifts—as they are called in the Bible—are define as follows:

- Knowledge—the facts (Proverbs 9:10, Proverbs 18:15, Colossians 2:8, 1 Timothy 2:4)
- Understanding—ability to translate meaning from the facts (Psalm 119:130; Proverbs 3:5–7, 18:2; Philippians 1:9–10)
- Wisdom—knowing what to do next, given an understanding of the facts and circumstances (Ecclesiastes 8:1, James 3:17)

Greek Nouns for *Know*

1. Gnosis: "primarily 'a seeking to know, an enquiry, investigation' . . . denotes, in the NT, 'knowledge,' especially of spiritual truth"
2. Epignosis: "denotes 'exact or full knowledge, discernment, recognition,' and is a strengthened form of gnosis, expressing a fuller or a full 'knowledge,' a greater participation by the 'knower' in the object 'known,' thus more powerfully influencing him. It is not found in the Gospels and acts. Paul uses it 15 times . . . out of the 20 occurrences."

Promise of the Holy Spirit

I will ask the Father, and He will give you another Helper, that He may be with you forever; that is the Spirit of truth, whom the world cannot receive, because it does not see Him or know Him, but you know Him because He abides with you and will be in you.

After a little while the world will no longer see Me, but you will see Me; because I live, you will live also. In that day you will know that I am in My Father, and you in Me, and I in you. He who has My commandments and keeps them is the one who loves Me; and he who loves Me will be loved by My Father, and I will love him and will disclose Myself to him.

These things I have spoken to you while abiding with you. But the Helper, the Holy Spirit, whom the Father will send in My name, He will teach you all things, and bring to your remembrance all that I said to you. (John 14:16–17, 19–21, 25–26 NASB)

Two Shall Become One
The only place in the physical world where two equals one is found in the spiritual world of relationships. We are taught this in scripture from the book of Genesis 2:24:

"Therefore a man shall leave his father and his mother and shall become united and cleave to his wife, and they shall become one flesh [Matthew 19:5, 1 Corinthians 6:16, Ephesians 5:31–33]" Genesis 2:24 AMPC.

Spiritual Mathematics

Paul declares, "But the person who is united to the Lord becomes one spirit with Him" (1 Corinthians 6:17).

"Do you not see and know that your bodies are members (bodily parts) of Christ (the Messiah)? Am I therefore to take the parts of Christ and make [them] parts of a prostitute? Never! Never! Or do you not know and realize that when a man joins himself to a prostitute, he becomes one body with her? The two, it is written, shall become one flesh [Genesis 2:24]. But the person who is united to the Lord becomes one spirit with Him. Shun immorality and all sexual looseness [flee from impurity in thought, word, or deed]. Any other sin which a man commits is one outside the body, but he who commits sexual immorality sins against his own body. Do you not know that your body is the temple (the very sanctuary) of the Holy Spirit Who lives within you, Whom you have received [as a Gift] from God? You are not your own, you were bought with a price [purchased with a preciousness and paid for, made His own]. So then, honor God and bring glory to Him in your body" (1 Corinthians 6:15–20 AMPC).

"But the one who joins himself to the Lord is one spirit with Him" (1 Corinthians 6:17 NASB)

Paul's Concern for the Galatian Believer

"O you poor and silly and thoughtless and unreflecting and senseless Galatians! Who has fascinated or bewitched or cast a spell over you, unto whom—right before your very eyes—Jesus Christ (the Messiah) was openly and graphically set forth and portrayed as crucified? Let me ask you this one question: Did you receive the [Holy] Spirit as the result of obeying the Law and doing its works, or was it by hearing [the message of the Gospel] and believing [it]? [Was it from observing a law of rituals or from a message of faith?] Are you so foolish and so senseless and so silly? Having begun [your new life spiritually] with the [Holy] Spirit, are you now reaching perfection [by dependence] on the flesh? Have you suffered so many things and experienced so much all for nothing (to no purpose)—if it really is to no purpose and in vain? Then does He Who supplies you with His marvelous [Holy] Spirit and works powerfully and miraculously among you do so on [the grounds of your doing] what the Law demands, or because of your believing in and adhering to and trusting in and relying on the message that you heard?" (Galatians 3:1–5 AMPC).

Who are the real sons and daughters of God?

"Not everyone who says to Me, Lord, Lord, will enter the kingdom of heaven, but he who does the will of My Father Who is in heaven" (Matthew 7:21 AMPC).

Jesus is just like you and me but in full submission to His Father: "Jesus of Nazareth, a Man attested by God to you by miracles, wonders, and signs which God did through Him in your midst" (Acts 2:22).

Jesus could not heal the sick. Neither could He deliver the tormented from demons or raise the dead. To believe otherwise is to ignore what He said about Himself and, more importantly, to miss the purpose of His self-imposed restriction to live as a man.

Jesus Christ said of Himself, "The Son can do nothing" (John 5:19). In the Greek language, the word *nothing* has a unique meaning—it means "nothing," just like it does in English! He had no supernatural capabilities whatsoever! While He is 100 percent God, He chose to live with the same limitations that man would face once he was redeemed. He made that point over and over again. Jesus became the model for all who would embrace the invitation to invade the impossible in His name. He performed miracles, wonders, and signs as a man in right relationship to God . . . not as God. If He performed miracles because He was God, then they would be unattainable for us.

"But if He did them as a man, I am responsible to pursue His lifestyle. Recapturing this simple truth changes everything . . . and makes possible a full restoration of the ministry of Jesus in His Church" (Bill Johnson, *When Heaven Invades Earth*).

What were the distinctions of His humanity?

1. He had no sin to separate Him from the Father.
2. He was completely dependent on the power of the Holy Spirit working through Him.

"Then Jesus, full of and controlled by the Holy Spirit, returned from the Jordan and was led in [the wilderness] [by] the [Holy] Spirit.

"Then Jesus went back full of and under the power of the [Holy] Spirit into Galilee, and the fame of Him spread through the whole region round about" (Luke 4:1, 14 AMPC).

What are the distinctions of our humanity?

1. We are sinners cleansed by the blood of Jesus. Through His sacrifice, He has successfully dealt with the power and effect of sin for all who believe. Nothing now separates us from the Father. There remains only one unsettled issue.
2. How dependent on the Holy Spirit are we willing to live?

"I assure you, most solemnly I tell you, if anyone steadfastly believes in Me, he will himself be able to do the things that I do; and he will do even greater things than these, because I go to the Father" (John 14:12 AMPC).

"I have strength for all things in Christ Who empowers me [I am ready for anything and equal to anything through Him Who infuses inner strength into me; I am self-sufficient in Christ's sufficiency]" (Philippians 4:13 AMPC).

"You are from God, little children, and have overcome them; because greater is He who is in you than he who is in the world" (1 John 4:4 AMPC).

"The kingdom of God is not a matter of talk but of power" (1 Corinthians 4:20 NIV).

"Seek first the kingdom of God" (Matthew 6:33).

Our faith has its anchor in the unseen realm. We as the sons and daughters of God live from the invisible toward the visible. Our faith actualizes what it realizes in the Kingdom of Heaven. The scriptures contrast the life of faith with the limitations of natural sight. Our faith provides eyes for our hearts to see the true reality of the spiritual world around us (Bill Johnson, *When Heaven Invades Earth*).

ETERNAL LIFE POINT: Position creates being, and being establishes the creative flow of fruit bearing. Fruit bearing is a natural process, flowing from the vine into its branches. The fruit bearing of the branches is created by the branch remaining or abiding in the vine.

"But when the time arrived that was set by God the Father, God sent his Son, born among us of a woman, born under the conditions of the law so that he might redeem those of us who have been kidnapped by the law. Thus we have been set free to experience our rightful heritage. You can tell for sure that you are now fully adopted as his own children because God sent the Spirit of his Son into our lives crying out, 'Papa! Father!' Doesn't that privilege of intimate conversation with God make it plain that you are not a slave, but a child? And if you are a child, you're also an heir, with complete access to the inheritance" (Galatians 4:4–7 MSG).

A Change of Thinking

"And do not be conformed to this world, but be transformed by the renewing of your mind, so that you may prove what the will of God is, that which is good and acceptable and perfect" (Romans 12:2 NASB).

"And that you be renewed in the spirit of your mind, and put on the new self, which in the likeness of God has been created in righteousness and holiness of the truth" (Ephesians 4:23–24 NASB).

ETERNAL LIFE POINT: Without the renewing of our minds and a clear understanding of the truth (the Word of God), we will continue to be enslaved to the rituals, traditions, and the elementary principles of this world, a slavery that is govern by the mindset of the flesh.

What does it mean to be of the mindset of the flesh, and what does it look like?

"For those who are according to the flesh set their minds on the things of the flesh" (Romans 8:5 NASB).

"Because the mind set on the flesh is hostile toward God; for it does not subject itself to the law of God, for it is not even able to do so, and those who are in the flesh cannot please God" (Romans 8:7–8 NASB).

We are no longer slaves to the traditions and elementary principles of this world, for scripture declares of the true sons and daughters of God:

"See to it that no one takes you captive through philosophy and empty deception, according to the tradition of men, according to the elementary principles of the world, rather than according to Christ" (Colossians 2:8 NASB).

Unbelief is anchored in what is visible or reasonable apart from God. It honors the natural realm as superior to the invisible. The apostle Paul states that what you can see is temporal and what you can't see is eternal. Unbelief is faith in the inferior.

ETERNAL LIFE POINT: The natural realm is the anchor of unbelief! (Bill Johnson, *The Supernatural Power of a Transformed Mind*).

God's life purpose: To show that every true son and daughter of God has full access to their supernatural inheritance in Christ so that they may bring Heaven's realities to earth, showing forth their Heavenly Father's glory as they honor Him through supernatural obedience.

ETERNAL LIFE POINT: Supernatural obedience is exercised through the renewed mindset of every true son and daughter of God by faith in the living truth of the Word of God.

As true heirs of the supernatural realities of the Kingdom of Heaven, every true believer is to exercise or practice their inheritance as the sons and daughters of God, giving life to all who would receive it around them.

You are God's Kingdom expression that thinks, that speaks, and that does Kingdom realities here on earth. We are called to bring the living presence of God's love to all of humanity.

"So, brethren, we [who are born again] are not children of a slave woman [the natural], but of the free [the supernatural]" (Galatians 4:31 AMPC).

Much of the Christian church in America has failed to take access of their supernatural inheritance through the renewing of their minds so that they could "be transformed (changed) by the [entire] renewal of their mind [by its new ideals and its new attitude], so that they may prove [for themselves] what is the good and acceptable and perfect will of God, even the thing which is good and acceptable and perfect [in His sight for them]" (Romans 12:2 AMPC).

ETERNAL LIFE POINT: What we focus on the most, we call into existence, whether it be from the mindset of the flesh or the mindset the Spirit.

Our freedom to choose creates our world around us! Will you choose the mindset of the flesh, which is death, or will you choose the mindset of the Spirit, which is life and peace, two becoming one?

The inheritance of every believer who would receive Jesus Christ is a life to the supernatural realities of the Kingdom of God—to be practiced in this world and in the world to come.

"But what does the Scripture say? Cast out and send away the slave woman and her son, for never shall the son of the slave woman be heir and share the inheritance with the son of the free woman [Genesis 21:10]. So, brethren, we [who are born again] are not children of a slave woman [the natural], but of the free [the supernatural]" (Galatians 4:30–31 AMPC).

You are the supernatural sons and daughters of God through the true vine Christ Jesus, and His branches and His divine fruit flow through us so that the world around us may be transformed and restored to the glory of God.

"Therefore if there is any encouragement in Christ, if there is any consolation of love, if there is any fellowship of the Spirit, if any affection and compassion, make my joy complete by being of the same mind, maintaining the same love, united in spirit, intent on one purpose" (Philippians 2:1–2 NASB).

We Are Born to Rule

In redeeming man, Jesus retrieved what man had given away. From the throne of triumph, He declared, "All authority has been given to Me in heaven and on earth. Go therefore" (Matthew 28:18–19). In other words, "I got it all back. Now go use it and reclaim mankind." In this passage, Jesus fulfills the promise He made to the disciples when He said, "I will give you the keys of the kingdom of heaven" (Matthew 16:19). The original plan was never aborted; it was fully realized once and for all in the resurrection and ascension of Jesus. We were then to be completely restored to His plan of ruling as people made in His image. And as such, we would learn how to enforce the victory obtained at Calvary. "The God of peace will soon crush Satan under your feet" (Romans 16:20 NIV).

We were born to rule—rule over creation, over darkness—to plunder hell and establish the rule of Jesus wherever we go by preaching the gospel of the Kingdom. *Kingdom* means "king's domain." In the original purpose of God, mankind ruled over creation. Now that sin has entered the world, creation has been infected by darkness—namely, disease, sickness, afflicting spirits, poverty, natural disasters, demonic influence, etc. Our rule is still over creation, but now it is focused on exposing and undoing the works of the devil. We are to give what we have received to reach that end (see Matthew 10:8).

If we truly receive power from an encounter with the God of power, we are more than equipped to give it away. The invasion of God into impossible situations comes through people who have received power from on high and learned to release it into the circumstances of life.

Jesus Speaks of His Oneness with the Father and with Us
When Jesus had spoken these things, He lifted up His eyes to heaven and said, Father, the hour has come. Glorify and exalt and honor and magnify your Son, so that your Son may glorify and extol and honor and magnify you. [Just as] you have granted Him power and authority over all flesh (all humankind), [now glorify Him] so that He may give eternal life to all whom you have given Him. And this is eternal life: [it means] to know (to perceive, recognize, become acquainted with, and understand) you, the only true and real God, and [likewise] to know Him, Jesus [as the] Christ (the anointed One, the Messiah), Whom you have sent. I have glorified you down here on the earth by completing the work that you gave Me to do.

And now, Father, glorify Me along with yourself and restore Me to such majesty and honor in your presence as I had with you before the world existed. I have manifested your Name [I have revealed your very Self, your real Self] to the people whom you have given Me out of the world.

They were yours, and you gave them to Me, and they have obeyed and kept your word.

Now [at last] they know and understand that all you have given Me belongs to you [is really and truly yours]. For the [uttered] words that you gave Me I have given them; and they have received and accepted [them] and have come to know positively and in reality [to believe with absolute assurance] that I came forth from your presence, and they have believed and are convinced that you did send Me. I am praying for them. I am not praying (requesting) for the world, but for those you have given Me, for they belong to you.

All [things that are] Mine are yours, and all [things that are] yours belong to Me; and I am glorified in (through) them. [They have done Me honor; in them My glory is achieved.] And [now] I am no more in the world, but these are [still] in the world, and I am coming to you. Holy Father, keep in your Name [in the knowledge of yourself] those whom you have given Me, that they may be one as We [are one].

While I was with them, I kept and preserved them in your Name [in the knowledge and worship of you]. Those you have given Me I guarded and protected, and not one of them has perished or is lost except the son of perdition [Judas Iscariot—the one who is now doomed to destruction, destined to be lost], that the Scripture might be fulfilled [Psalm 41:9, John 6:70].

And now I am coming to you; I say these things while I am still in the world, so that My joy may be made full and complete and perfect in them [that they may experience My delight fulfilled in them, that My enjoyment may be perfected in their own souls, that they may have My gladness within them, filling their hearts]. I have given and delivered to them your word (message) and the world has hated them, because they are not of the world [do not belong to the world], just as I am not of the world.

I do not ask that you will take them out of the world, but that you will keep and protect them from the evil one. They are not of the world (worldly, belonging to the world), [just] as I am not of the world. Sanctify them [purify, consecrate, separate them for yourself, make them holy] by the truth; your Word is truth. Just as you sent Me into the world, I also have sent them into the world. And so for their sake and on their behalf I sanctify (dedicate, consecrate) Myself, that they also may be sanctified (dedicated, consecrated, made holy) in the truth.

Neither for these alone do I pray [it is not for their sake only that I make this request], but also for all those who will ever come to believe in (trust in, cling to, rely on) Me through their word and teaching, that they all may be one, [just] as you, Father, are in Me and I in you, that they also may be one in Us, so that the world may believe and be convinced that you have sent Me.

I have given to them the glory and honor which you have given Me, that they may be one [even] as We are one: I in them and you in Me, in order that they may become one and perfectly united, that the world may know and [definitely] recognize that you sent Me and that you have loved them [even] as you have loved Me. Father, I desire that they also whom you have entrusted to Me [as your gift to Me] may be with Me where I am, so that they may see My glory, which you have given Me [your love gift to Me]; for you loved Me before the foundation of the world.

O just and righteous Father, although the world has not known you and has failed to recognize you and has never acknowledged you, I have known you [continually]; and these men understand and know that you have sent Me. I have made your Name known to them and revealed your character and your very Self, and I will continue to make [you] known, that the love which you have bestowed upon Me may be in them [felt in their hearts] and that I [Myself] may be in them. (John 17:1–26 AMPC)

ETERNAL LIFE POINT: There is no Kingdom realities without oneness with the Lord.

"But the person who is united to the Lord becomes one spirit with Him" (1 Corinthians 6:17 AMPC).

ETERNAL LIFE POINT: Walking in our oneness begins now, and loving like our Heavenly Father is our inheritance to display His honor and glory to the world around us.

Life Application

1. How often do you feel as one with Christ Jesus?
2. Why is it important to live in oneness with Christ Jesus?
3. Are Heaven realities a part of who you are?
4. What's your life application from this teaching?

Concentrate and Meditate on These Words

Dear friends, listen well to my words. Keep my message in plain view at all times. Concentrate! Learn it by heart! Those who discover these words live, really live; body and soul, they're bursting with health. Keep vigilant watch over your heart; that's where life starts. (Proverbs 4:20–23 Message Bible)

God calls us friends; He has five commands:

1. Listen well to His Words.
2. Tune your ears to His voice.
3. Keep His message in plain view at all times.
4. Concentrate on it (intentional internal focused faith).
5. Learn it by heart (memorize it),

Promise to be fulfilled for those who practice these Words: they will live, really live (abundantly), and their bodies and souls will be bursting with health.

Chapter 12

A FREEDOM BEYOND COMPREHENSION

I will not be speaking by the spirit of the world or the mind of the flesh, but I will be speaking from the mind of the Spirit who is from God, so that we may know the things freely given to us by God, which things I will also speak, not in words taught by human wisdom, but in those taught by the Spirit, combining spiritual thoughts with spiritual words.
—1 Corinthians 2:12–13 NASB

As for you, the anointing which you received from Him abides in you, and you have no need for anyone to teach you; but as His anointing teaches you about all things, and is true and is not a lie, and just as it has taught you, you abide in Him.
—1 John 2:27 NASB

ETERNAL LIFE POINT: Every believer must have the infilling of the Holy Spirit so that she or he can understand the spiritual thought and spiritual words from God. Everything in God must come and be revealed through the mindset of the Holy Spirit.

God's purpose: To show that a true follower of Jesus Christ can live a life free from the power of sin and death as they become the spiritual reality (in Christ) that is manifested in and through their physical earth suits. Their position and identity must always be in Christ, for they now are His Body (presence on earth) while He remains the head of His church.

ETERNAL LIFE POINT: To show that it is absolutely imperative that each believer must maintain his or her position in Christ and make Christ Jesus their identity while putting to death the deeds of their flesh. For believers no longer lives for the dictates and appetites of their flesh but for the will of God.

Question: Where do our deeds of the flesh come from, and what are they really?

There are two sides to this double question that all starts from our emotional thought life.

When something happens to us that creates uncomfortableness, it becomes an out-of-our-control situation or circumstance and goes against our fleshly appetite that now triggers our emotional senses, which respond by creating an attitude or mindset. This attitude or mindset becomes a Goliath that starts each day with taunts and ends each day with taunts. As time goes by, all that demoralizing and diminishing has had an effect on us. We began to believe, in spite of our best efforts, something undesirable was going to happen to us . . . our defeat.

"So, since Christ suffered in the flesh for us, (for you), arm yourselves with the same thought and purpose [patiently to suffer rather than fail to please God]. For whoever has suffered in the flesh [having the mind of Christ] is done with [intentional] sin [has stopped pleasing himself and the world, and pleases God], so that he can no longer spend the rest of his natural life living by [his] human appetites and desires, but [he lives] for what God wills" (1 Peter 4:1–2 AMPC).

ETERNAL LIFE POINT: Every believer is called and purposed to suffer in the flesh for the sake of Christ in behalf of others.

Listening to Scripture

"Therefore there is now no condemnation for those who are in Christ Jesus. For the law of the Spirit of life in Christ Jesus has set you free from the law of sin and of death. For what the Law could not do, weak as it was through the flesh, God did: sending His own Son in the likeness of sinful flesh and as an offering for sin, He condemned sin in the flesh, so that the requirement of the Law might be fulfilled in us, who do not walk according to the flesh but according to the Spirit" (Romans 8:1–4 NASB).

"For the death that He died, He died to sin once for all; but the life that He lives, He lives to God. Even so consider yourselves to be dead to sin, but alive to God in Christ Jesus" (Romans 6:10–11 NASB).

ETERNAL LIFE POINT: There is no life outside the believer's position in Christ.

"Since you have been raised to new life with Christ, set your sights on the realities of heaven, where Christ sits in the place of honor at God's right hand. Think about the things of heaven, not the things of earth. For you died to this life, and your real life is hidden with Christ in God. And when Christ, who is your life, is revealed to the whole world, you will share in all his glory. So put to death the sinful, earthly things lurking within you. Have nothing to do with sexual immorality, impurity, lust, and evil desires. Don't be greedy, for a greedy person is an idolater, worshiping the things of this world. Because of these sins, the anger of God is coming. You used to do these things when your life was still part of this world. But now is the time to get rid of anger, rage, malicious behavior, slander, and dirty language. Don't lie to each other, for you have stripped off your old sinful nature and all its wicked deeds. Put on your new nature, and be renewed as you learn to know your Creator and become like him" (Colossians 3:1–10 NLT).

Victory over the Flesh

"So then, brethren, we are debtors, but not to the flesh [we are not obligated to our carnal nature], to live [a life ruled by the standards set up by the dictates] of the flesh" (Romans 8:12 AMPC).

"So then, brethren, we are under obligation, not to the flesh, to live according to the flesh" (Romans 8:12 NASB).

"Therefore, brethren, we are debtors—not to the flesh, to live according to the flesh" (Romans 8:12 NKJV).

"Therefore, dear brothers and sisters, you have no obligation to do what your sinful nature urges you to do" (Romans 8:12 NLT).

"So don't you see that we don't owe this old do-it-yourself life one red cent. There's nothing in it for us, nothing at all. The best thing to do is give it a decent burial and get on with your new life. God's Spirit beckons. There are things to do and places to go!" (Romans 8:12–14 MSG).

"For I through the Law [under the operation of the curse of the Law] have [in Christ's death for me] myself died to the Law and all the Law's demands upon me, so that I may [henceforth] live to and for God. I have been crucified with Christ [in Him I have shared His crucifixion]; it is no longer I who live, but Christ (the Messiah) lives in me; and the life I now live in the body I live by faith in (by adherence to and reliance on and complete trust in) the Son of God, Who loved me and gave Himself up for me. [Therefore, I do not treat God's gracious gift as something of minor importance and defeat its very purpose]; I do not set aside and invalidate and frustrate and nullify the grace (unmerited favor) of God. For if justification (righteousness, acquittal from guilt) comes through [observing the ritual of] the Law, then Christ (the Messiah) died groundlessly and to no purpose and in vain. [His death was then wholly superfluous.]" (Galatians 2:19–21 AMPC).

"For those who are according to the flesh and are controlled by its unholy desires set their minds on and pursue those things which gratify the flesh, but those who are according to the Spirit and are controlled by the desires of the Spirit set their minds on and seek those things which gratify the [Holy] Spirit. Now the mind of the flesh [which is sense and reason without the Holy Spirit] is death [death that comprises all the miseries arising from sin, both here and hereafter]. But the mind of the [Holy] Spirit is life and [soul] peace [both now and forever]. [That is] because the mind of the flesh [with its carnal thoughts and purposes] is hostile to God, for it does not submit itself to God's Law; indeed it cannot. So then those who are living the life of the flesh [catering to the appetites and impulses of their carnal nature] cannot please or satisfy God, or be acceptable to Him. But you are not living the life of the flesh, you are living the life of the Spirit, if the [Holy] Spirit of God [really] dwells within you [directs and controls you]. But if anyone does not possess the [Holy] Spirit of Christ, he is none of His [he does not belong to Christ, is not truly a child of God] [Romans 8:14]. But if Christ lives in you, [then although] your [natural] body is dead by reason of sin and guilt, the spirit is alive because of [the] righteousness [that He imputes to you]. And if the Spirit of Him Who raised up Jesus from the dead dwells in you, [then] He Who raised up Christ Jesus from the dead will also restore to life your mortal (short-lived, perishable) bodies through His Spirit Who dwells in you. So then, brethren, we are debtors, but not to the flesh [we are not obligated to our carnal nature], to live [a life ruled by the standards set up by the dictates] of the flesh. For if you live according to [the dictates of] the flesh, you will surely die. But if through the power of the [Holy] Spirit you are [habitually] putting to death (making extinct, deadening) the [evil] deeds prompted by the body, you shall [really and genuinely] live forever. For all who are led by the Spirit of God are sons of God" (Romans 8:5–14 AMPC).

ETERNAL LIFE POINT: The believer's position and identity are spiritual realities made possible through the death and resurrection of Jesus Christ, for every believer was in Christ when He went to the cross and when He arose from the dead.

ETERNAL LIFE POINT: As believers in Jesus Christ, our lived lives on planet earth is now found in Christ Who has now become our real life as we live this spiritual reality in and through these physical earth suits; we are declaring and displaying Heaven's reality on earth in our words, deeds, and thoughts by the power of God (Holy Spirit) to His honor and His glory.

Can I really be free from sin?

Complete freedom from sin—isn't that impossible?

According to popular opinion, it is impossible to become free from sin. Sin is anything that goes against God's will and His laws. To commit sin is to transgress or disobey these laws. The lust to sin dwells in human nature. In other words, it is contaminated and motivated by the sinful tendencies that dwell in all people as a result of the fall into sin and disobedience in the Garden of Eden.

Question: What is Christian freedom?

Answer: The Bible states emphatically in Galatians 5:1 that believers are free in Christ: "It is for freedom that Christ has set us free" (Galatians 5:1). Before Jesus died on the cross, God's people lived under a detailed system of laws that served as a moral compass to guide their lives. The Law, while powerless to grant salvation or produce true freedom, nevertheless pointed the way to Jesus Christ (Galatians 3:19–24). Through His sacrificial death, Jesus Christ fulfilled the Law, setting believers free from the law of sin and death. God's laws are now written in our hearts through the Spirit of God, and we are free to follow and serve Christ in ways that please and glorify Him (Romans 8:2–8). In a nutshell, this is the definition of Christian freedom.

An important aspect of Christian freedom is our responsibility not to return to living under the Law. The apostle Paul compared this to slavery: "Stand firm, then, and do not let yourselves be burdened again by a yoke of slavery" (Galatians 5:1). Continuing to live under the Law after salvation is merely a legalistic form of religion. We cannot earn righteousness through the Law; rather, the Law's purpose was to define our sin and show our need of a savior. Christian freedom involves living not under the burdensome obligations of the Law but under God's grace: "For sin shall no longer be your master, because you are not under the law, but under grace" (Romans 6:14).

In Christ, we are free from the Law's oppressive system, we are free from the penalty of sin, and we are free from the power of sin. Christian freedom is not a license to sin. We are free in Christ but not free to live however we want, indulging the flesh: "For you have been called to live in freedom, my brothers and sisters. But don't use your freedom to satisfy your sinful nature. Instead, use your freedom to serve one another in love" (Galatians 5:13 NLT). Believers aren't free to sin but free to live holy lives in Christ.

Christian freedom is one of the many paradoxes of the Christian faith. True freedom means willingly becoming a slave to Christ, and this happens through relationship with Him (Colossians 2:16–17). In Romans 6, Paul explains that when a believer accepts Christ, he or she is baptized by the Spirit into Christ's death, burial, and resurrection. At that moment, the believer ceases to be a slave to sin and becomes a servant of righteousness. "But thanks be to God, that you who were once slaves of sin have become obedient from the heart to the standard of teaching to which you were committed, and, having been set free from sin, have become slaves of righteousness" (Romans 6:17–18 ESV).

Only Christians know true freedom: "If the Son sets you free, you will be free indeed" (John 8:36). But what does Christian freedom look like in a practical sense? What are we free to do and not do? What can we watch on TV? What can we eat and drink? What can we wear to the beach? What about smoking and drinking? Are there limits to Christian freedom?

In 1 Corinthians 10, the apostle Paul gives a practical illustration of

Christian freedom: "'Everything is permissible'—but not everything is beneficial. 'Everything is permissible'—but not everything is constructive. Nobody should seek his own good, but the good of others" (1 Corinthians 10:23–24).

In writing to the church in Corinth, Paul mentions members who were attending meals in pagan temples, just as they had done before receiving Christ. They felt free to continue participating because they thought these festivals were merely a normal part of the social culture. They didn't see their actions as pagan worship. Paul laid out several warnings, reminding the Corinthians of Israel's dangerous flirtation with idolatry in the Old Testament. Then he handled the practical concern of eating meat that had been sacrificed to idols.

"Everything is permissible," the Corinthians were saying. "True," Paul says, "Christians have a great deal of freedom in Christ. However, not everything is beneficial or constructive. Our freedom in Christ must be balanced by a desire to build up and benefit others. When deciding how to exercise our Christian freedom, we ought to seek the good of others before our own good."

In Judaism, restrictions were placed on purchasing meats in the market. Jews could only buy and eat kosher meats. Paul said believers were free in Christ to buy and eat any meat (1 Corinthians 10:25–26). However, if the issue of meat sacrificed to idols came up, believers were to follow a higher law. Love is what limits Christian freedom.

A little later in the chapter, Paul wrote about eating meat as a guest in someone's home. Christians are free to eat whatever they are served without questions of conscience (1 Corinthians 10:27). But if someone brings up that the meat has been offered to an idol, it is better not to eat it for the sake of the person who raised the issue of conscience (verse 28). While believers have freedom to eat the meat, they are compelled to consider what's best for those who are observing their behavior.

Romans 14:1–13 raises a key determiner in understanding the limits of Christian freedom. In the passage, Paul again brings up the issue of eating meat sacrificed to idols and also observing certain holy days. Some of the believers felt freedom in Christ in these areas, while others did not. Their differing perspectives were causing quarrels and disunity. Paul emphasized that unity and love in the body of Christ are more important than anyone's personal convictions or Christian liberty: "Therefore let us stop passing judgment on one another. Instead, make up your mind not to put any stumbling block or obstacle in the way of a brother or sister" (Romans 14:13).

Essentially, Paul's message to the New Testament believers and to us today is this: even if we believe we are right and have Christian freedom in an area, if our actions will cause another brother or sister to stumble in his or her faith, we are to refrain out of love.

Paul spoke again of the matter in 1 Corinthians 8:7–9: "Some people are still so accustomed to idols that when they eat sacrificial food they think of it as having been sacrificed to a god, and since their conscience is weak, it is defiled. But food does not bring us near to God; we are no worse if we do not eat, and no better if we do. Be careful, however, that the exercise of your rights does not become a stumbling block to the weak."

The issue in New Testament times was eating meat offered to idols; today there are other gray areas that arise in our Christian walk. Romans 14:1 calls these disputable matters, areas where the Bible does not give clear-cut guidelines on whether a behavior is sin. When we are faced with gray areas, we can rely on two guiding principles to regulate our Christian freedom: let love for others compel us not to cause anyone to stumble, and let our desire to glorify God be our all-encompassing motive (1 Corinthians 10:31).

ETERNAL LIFE POINT: God's Word and commands cannot be viewed as regulations or as law for a believer; they must be seen through the eyes of relationship. We cannot know God through commands and rules. We will find no intimacy in regulations and rules.

Two Kinds of Freedom
This example also indicates that there are actually two kinds of freedom from sin:

1. The first is liberation from the law of sin and death (Romans 8:2). In Colossians 2:11, it is written that we have put off "the body of the sins of the flesh" (that body that committed sin and served sin) by the circumcision of Christ. In other words, we choose to stop committing conscious sin. This is the first freedom.

2. The second freedom is a process—a growth—whereby we are gradually liberated from "the law of sin in our members." The second freedom occurs gradually, as it is written in Philippians 3:7–16. This liberation is the process of being made perfect.

The desires that we experience that go against God's will is a desire for anything sinful (see James 1:14), also called sin in the flesh. Although the expression "youthful lusts" is often thought of in connection with sinful sexual desires, lusts also include anything that goes against what is good and right in God's eyes (2 Timothy 2:22).

What should we do?

The only way to be finished with sin in the flesh is to go the same way that Jesus went. It is written that He is our forerunner, and He opened this way through the flesh for us to follow Him.

"For you have been called for this purpose, since Christ also suffered for you, leaving you an example for you to follow in His steps, WHO COMMITTED NO SIN, NOR WAS ANY DECEIT FOUND IN HIS MOUTH; and while being reviled, He did not revile in return; while suffering, He uttered no threats, but kept entrusting Himself to Him who judges righteously; and He Himself bore our sins in His body on the cross, so that we might die to sin and live to righteousness; for by His wounds you were healed" (1 Peter 2:21–24 NASB).

"Therefore, since Christ has suffered in the flesh, arm yourselves also with the same purpose, because he who has suffered in the flesh has ceased from sin, so as to live the rest of the time in the flesh no longer for the lusts of men, but for the will of God" (1 Peter 4:1–2 NASB).

ETERNAL LIFE POINT: Living from position and identity is a given spiritual reality by the life and empowerment of the Holy Spirit for every believer who would choose to walk by faith in Christ as they put to death there sinful fleshly mindset and live by the mindset of the Spirit.

Our freedom is greater than our ability to comprehend! Our flesh has been crucified in Christ Jesus, and we are now free from self-abatement and man-made rules, and we now live by one law—the law of love.

"And in Him you were also circumcised with a circumcision made without hands, in the removal of the body of the flesh by the circumcision of Christ; having been buried with Him in baptism, in which you were also raised up with Him through faith in the working of God, who raised Him from the dead. When you were dead in your transgressions and the uncircumcision of your flesh, He made you alive together with Him, having forgiven us all our transgressions, having canceled out the certificate of debt consisting of decrees against us, which was hostile to us; and He has taken it out of the way, having nailed it to the cross. When He had disarmed the rulers and authorities, He made a public display of them, having triumphed over them through Him. Therefore no one is to act as your judge in regard to food or drink or in respect to a festival or a new moon or a Sabbath day—things which are a mere shadow of what is to come; but the substance belongs to Christ. Let no one keep defrauding you of your prize by delighting in self-abasement and the worship of the angels, taking his stand on visions he has seen, inflated without cause by his fleshly mind, and not holding fast to the head, from whom the entire body, being supplied and held together by the joints and ligaments, grows with a growth which is from God. If you have died with Christ to the elementary principles of the world, why, as if you were living in the world, do you submit yourself to decrees, such as, "Do not handle, do not taste, do not touch!" (which all refer to things destined to perish with use)—in accordance with the commandments and teachings of men? These are matters which have, to be sure, the appearance of wisdom in self-made religion and self-abasement and severe treatment of the body, but are of no value against fleshly indulgence" (Colossians 2:11–23 NASB).

ETERNAL LIFE POINT: Every believer must take their created position in Christ Jesus, the full expression of the love of God.

Life Application

1. What do you understand this chapter to be saying about your life in Christ?
2. How do you or have you overcome the power of sin and death in your life?
3. What's your life application takeaway from this chapter?
4. Write a prayer that can become your intentional internal focused faith from this chapter.

Concentrate and Meditate on These Words

Dear friends, listen well to my words. Keep my message in plain view at all times. Concentrate! Learn it by heart! Those who discover these words live, really live; body and soul, they're bursting with health. Keep vigilant watch over your heart; that's where life starts. (Proverbs 4:20–23 Message Bible)

God calls us friends; He has five commands:

1. Listen well to His Words.
2. Tune your ears to His voice.
3. Keep His message in plain view at all times.
4. Concentrate on it (intentional internal focused faith).
5. Learn it by heart (memorize it).

Promise to be fulfilled for those who practice these Words: they will live, really live (abundantly), and their bodies and souls will be bursting with health.

Chapter 13

LISTENING TO GOD'S VOICE

ETERNAL LIFE POINT: Every believer must have the spiritual ear of the Holy Spirit to know the voice of their Master. Yet at the same time, Jesus said, "My sheep hear My voice" in John 10:27. Jesus is the Living Word, speaking the heart of the Father. God has chosen to speak to us through His Son (Hebrews 1:2). This is a promise available to us. Yet at the same time, I don't meet a lot of people who have been personally taught how to listen to God in an effective and practical way. Too many people wing it but get easily discouraged.

Tuning Your Listening

The fact is, we are listening to thoughts all day long, so we have to determine what we will listen to. If we want to hear from God, then it's important that we tune our listening to hearing Him.

What we listen to determines a lot of things in our lives. We need to be intentional about what we listen to and how we listen so that we can tune ourselves more to what God is saying and what He is saying over our lives.

ETERNAL LIFE POINT: Silent words are spoken words listened to and acted upon by all of humanity, whether negatively or positively.

Learning to Listen to God

Hearing from God and allowing ourself to be empowered by His thoughts toward us is one of the most valuable exercises we'll ever do. Listening to God can be a daily habit that will change each one of our lives. But we all need some help and enhancement so that we are tuning in to the frequency of Heaven over our lives.

Canceling out extraneous noise is needful in society these days. We receive a constant barrage of messages, calls, notifications, and environmental cues that overload our brains. It overwhelms me so much so that when it is quiet, it takes my thoughts a long time to quiet down.

The noise in my brain (and heart) contributes to my inability to hear God clearly. My physical hearing is overloaded, which then affects my spiritual ears, making it tough for me to hear the still, small voice of God. But life beckons me onward, and I do my zombie shuffle with spiritual ears that aren't working at full capacity. Just like how those earbuds cancel out the din of life, so does zombie-like faith cancel out the whispers of God that bring me true life. I need to hear from God to live and live well.

Several times Jesus told the people around Him something like this: "If anyone has ears to hear, let him hear" (Mark 4:9, 23; Luke 8:8, 14:35). Spiritual hearing is something we need to practice. These are spiritual muscles, so to speak, ones that need conditioning. And since every one of us has ears, Jesus is inviting every one of us to give it a try.

I've noticed that a steady intake of noise from the world dampens my interest in seeking the quiet I need to tune my ears to hear God's voice. I have to make space for it—sort of like popping in my noise-cancelling earbuds. Silence isn't just going to happen naturally. You have to choose it and make it happen.

Our scripture this week has been John 10:27. Jesus said, "My sheep hear My voice and I know them and they follow Me." Jesus also made the statement that the sheep won't follow a stranger's voice. Why does the sheep recognize the shepherd's voice over the stranger's voice? It's not that complicated of an answer. Because of constantly being around the shepherd and hearing the shepherd's voice, they know his voice over any other.

It's the same with our children. I guarantee if you were to take a mother into a room full of kids, that mother could audibly pick out their own child over all the other voices. Why? Because that mother has been with her child so much, her ears are fine-tuned to their child's voice.

Just like that crowded room of kids, we live in a crowded world full of voices vying for our attention. If you want to fine-tune your ear to God's voice, the answer is simple: spend time with Him.

1.   Good listening requires patience.

Here Bonhoeffer gives us something to avoid: "a kind of listening with half an ear that presumes already to know what the other person has to say." This, he says, "is an impatient, inattentive listening, that . . . is only waiting for a chance to speak." Perhaps we think we know where the speaker is going, and so we already begin formulating our response. Or we are in the middle of something when someone starts talking to us, or we have another commitment approaching and we wish they were done already. Or maybe we're half-eared because our attention is divided by our external surroundings or our internal rebounding to self. As Dunn laments, "Unfortunately, many of us are too preoccupied with ourselves when we listen. Instead of concentrating on what is being said, we are busy either deciding what to say in response or mentally rejecting the other person's point of view."

"Poor listening diminishes another person, while good listening invites them to exist and matter."

Positively, then, good listening requires concentration and means we're in with both ears and that we hear the other person out till they're done speaking. Rarely will the speaker begin with what's most important and deepest. We need to hear the whole train of thought, all the way to the caboose, before starting across the tracks.

Good listening silences the smartphone and doesn't stop the story and is attentive and patient—externally relaxed and internally active. It takes energy to block out the distractions that keep bombarding us and the peripheral things that keep streaming into our consciousness and the many good possibilities we can spin out for interrupting. When we are people quick to speak, it takes Spirit-powered patience to not only be quick to hear but to also keep on hearing.

2.   Good listening is an act of love.

Half-eared listening, says Bonhoeffer, "despises the brother and is only waiting for a chance to speak and thus get rid of the other person."

Poor listening rejects; good listening embraces. Poor listening diminishes the other person, while good listening invites them to exist and to matter. Bonhoeffer writes, "Just as love to God begins with listening to his Word, so the beginning of love for the brethren is learning to listen to them."

Good listening goes hand in hand with the mindset of Christ (Philippians 2:5).

"Let this same attitude and purpose and [humble] mind be in you which was in Christ Jesus: [Let Him be your example in humility:]" (Philippians 2:5 AMPC).

It flows from a humble heart that counts others more significant than ourselves (Philippians 2:3). It looks not only to its own interests but also the interests of others (Philippians 2:4). It is patient and kind (1 Corinthians 13:4).

3.   Good listening asks perceptive questions.

This counsel is writ large in the Proverbs. It is the fool who "takes no pleasure in understanding, but only in expressing his opinion" (Proverbs 18:2) and thus "gives an answer before he hears" (Proverbs 13:2). "The purpose in a man's heart is like deep water," says Proverbs 20:5, "but a man of understanding will draw it out."

Good listening asks perceptive, open-ended questions that don't tee up yes-no answers but gently peel the onion and probe beneath the surface. It watches carefully for nonverbal communication but doesn't interrogate and pry into details the speaker doesn't want to share and meekly draws them out and helps point the speaker to fresh perspectives through careful but genuine questions.

4.   Good listening is ministry.

According to Bonhoeffer, there are many times when "listening can be a greater service than speaking." God wants more of the Christian than just our good listening, but not less. There will be days when the most important ministry we do is square our shoulders to some hurting person, uncross our arms, lean forward, make eye contact, and hear their pain all the way to the bottom. Says Dunn, good listening often defuses the emotions that are a part of the problem being discussed. Sometimes releasing these emotions is all that is needed to solve the problem. The speaker may neither want nor expect us to say anything in response.

One of Dunn's counsels for cultivating good listening is this: "put more emphasis on affirmation than on answers . . . [m]any times God simply wants to use me as a channel of his affirming love as I listen with compassion and understanding." Echoes Bonhoeffer, "Often a person can be helped merely by having someone who will listen to him seriously." At times, what our neighbor needs most is for someone else to know.

5.   Good listening prepares us to speak well.

"The best ministry you might do today is to listen to someone's pain all the way to the bottom." Have you ever gone to the bottom of someone's pain by listening to them?

Sometimes good listening only listens and ministers best by keeping quiet, but typically, good listening readies us to minister words of grace to precisely the place where the other is in need. As Bonhoeffer writes, "We should listen with the ears of God that we may speak the Word of God."

While the fool "gives an answer before he hears" (Proverbs 18:13), the wise person tries to resist defensiveness and to listen from a nonjudgmental stance, training himself not to formulate opinions or responses until the full update is on the table and the whole story has been heard.

6.   Good listening reflects our relationship with God.

Our inability to listen well to others may be symptomatic of a chatty spirit that is droning out the voice of God.

"Whoever is of God listens to God. [Those who belong to God hear the words of God.] This is the reason that you do not listen [to those words, to Me]: because you do not belong to God and are not of God or in harmony with Him" (John 8:47 AMPC).

Let this not be you or me who do not listen to the voice of our Lord and King as we are led by our empowering Holy Spirit.

ETERNAL LIFE POINT: It's an eternal requirement to know the voice of the Lord Jesus Christ.

"The sheep that are My own hear and are listening to My voice; and I know them, and they follow Me" (John 10:27 AMPC).

Bonhoeffer warns, "He who can no longer listen to his brother will soon be no longer listening to God either; he will be doing nothing but prattle in the presence of God too. This is the beginning of the death of the spiritual life . . . anyone who thinks that his time is too valuable to spend keeping quiet will eventually have no time for God and his brother, but only for himself and for his own follies." (Most of these thoughts are someone I do not know, in this chapter, but I believe in the spiritual reality of these words.)

Good listening is a great means of grace in the dynamic of true Christian fellowship. Not only is it a channel through which God continues to pour his grace into our lives but it's also His way of using us as His means of grace in the lives of others. It may be one of the hardest things we learn to do, but we will find it worth every ounce of effort.

ETERNAL LIFE POINT: Good listening is the first step to intentional internal focused faith that leads to adhering to, trusting in, and relying upon the full work of grace for Heaven's realities in the eternal moment of now.

Life Application

1. Are you a good listener? If so, how and what did you do to become a good listener?
2. Why is it important to know the voice of the Master?
3. What is your most difficulty in listening?
4. What's your life application from this teaching?
5. Write a prayer that you can develop intentional internal focused faith upon in your ability to listen.

Concentrate and Meditate on These Words

Dear friends, listen well to my words. Keep my message in plain view at all times. Concentrate! Learn it by heart! Those who discover these words live, really live; body and soul, they're bursting with health. Keep vigilant watch over your heart; that's where life starts. (Proverbs 4:20–23 Message Bible)

God calls us friends; He has five commands:

1. Listen well to His Words.
2. Tune your ears to His voice.
3. Keep His message in plain view at all times.
4. Concentrate on it (intentional internal focused faith).
5. Learn it by heart (memorize it).

Promise to be fulfilled for those who practice these Words: they will live, really live (abundantly), and their bodies and souls will be healthy.

Conclusion

But don't just listen to God's word. You must do what it says. Otherwise, you are only fooling yourselves. For if you listen to the word and don't obey, it is like glancing at your face in a mirror. You see yourself, walk away, and forget what you look like. But if you look carefully into the perfect law that sets you free, and if you do what it says and don't forget what you heard, then God will bless you for doing it. (James 1:22–25 NLT)

ETERNAL LIFE POINT: mere talk is just what it is, just words with no substance that leads only to emptiness and vapor.

The discipline of practicing the renewing of our minds creates an attitude of hard work and fulling blessings. It is a great thing to set down and write out your goals and to establish your plans. All point to wonderful desires, but desires alone profit nothing without the will to practice what you desire.

Jesus said, "Keep watching and praying that you may not come into temptation; the spirit is willing, but the flesh is weak" (Mark 14:38 NASB).

If there is no continuous practicing of walking out the truth by the life of the Spirit, there can be no heavenly realities to give evidence of a transformed life in Christ Jesus.

Yours and my faith create Heaven's realities that become profitable and beneficiary for all who would dare to believe the witness of our transformed lives. This is why the renewing of mind and heart is a must for every follower of Jesus Christ, because we each becomes a living example of truth and not just a vapor of hot air.

Concentrate and Meditate on These Words

Dear friends, listen well to my words. Keep my message in plain view at all times. Concentrate! Learn it by heart! Those who discover these words live, really live; body and soul, they're bursting with health. Keep vigilant watch over your heart; that's where life starts. (Proverbs 4:20–23 Message Bible)

God calls us friends; He has five commands:

1. Listen well to His Words.
2. Tune your ears to His voice.
3. Keep His message in plain view at all times.
4. Concentrate on it (intentional internal focused faith).
5. Learn it by heart (memorize it).

Promise to be fulfilled for those who practice these Words: they will live, really live (abundantly), and their bodies and souls will be bursting with health.

1. Write for yourself a life application.
2. Memorize the scripture (intentional internal focused faith).
3. Write a prayer from your life application to practice daily.
4. Practice living the truth of your prayer daily.

Chapter 14

KOINONIA, THE TRUE EARMARK
OF FELLOWSHIP

There can be no true fellowship (koinonia) with one another unless we have true intimacy (koinonia) with Jesus Christ.

All relationships grow and flow from what and whom we worship!

Two Fellowships Equal One

If we don't have true intimacy (koinonia) with our Heavenly Father, we cannot develop true koinonia (fellowship) with our fellow man. In other words, true fellowship with our Heavenly Father creates true fellowship with our brothers and sisters in Christ Jesus. All relationships that we have must first start with our Creator and Maker before we can have true fellowship with the family of God.

"The Promises of God are like the rudder to a ship. Reviewing them sets the direction for our whole life."

"How can a young person live a clean life? By carefully reading the map of your Word. I'm single-minded in pursuit of you; don't let me miss the road signs you've posted. I've banked your promises in the vault of my heart so I won't sin myself bankrupt. Be blessed, GOD; train me in your ways of wise living. I'll transfer to my lips all the counsel that comes from your mouth; I delight far more in what you tell me about living than in gathering a pile of riches. I ponder every morsel of wisdom from you, I attentively watch how you've done it. I relish everything you've told me of life, I won't forget a word of it" (Psalm 119:9–16 MSG).

This scripture defines for us a true picture of what fellowship (koinonia) truly is. It's a picture of one having intimacy with God and nothing else compares to their relationship. Does this picture describe your intimacy and fellowship with Jesus Christ?

Concentrate and Meditate on These Words
Dear friends, listen well to my words. Keep my message in plain view at all times. Concentrate! Learn it by heart! Those who discover these words live, really live; body and soul, they're bursting with health. Keep vigilant watch over your heart; that's where life starts. (Proverbs 4:20–23 Message Bible)

God calls us friends; He has five commands:

1. Listen well to His Words.
2. Tune your ears to His voice.
3. Keep His message in plain view at all times.
4. Concentrate on it (intentional internal focused faith).
5. Learn it by heart (memorize it).

An intimacy with your Heavenly Father is created. Promise to be fulfilled for those who practice these Words: they will live, really live (abundantly), and their bodies and souls will be bursting with health.

Meditation Done Right
Intentional internal focused faith creates intimacy with your Heavenly Father (this is single-mindedness).

In Eastern occult religions, meditation means emptying the mind. But biblical meditation is the opposite—it's filling the mind with God's truth.

Some Christians don't like the idea of meditation because they've only seen it or heard about it being demonstrated in a corrupt way through diabolical religions.

But if you've ever worried about something, you already know how to meditate! Every person, saint, and sinner alike meditate every day.

The question is, What are you meditating on? Meditation is intentional internal focus on something or someone.

Apostle Paul declares, "And my God will supply all your needs according to His riches in glory in Christ Jesus" (Philippians 4:19 NASB).

But you say, "I got a problem with my finances." A person with a renewed mind derives joy even in that circumstance because joy comes not by what is seen but by what God says. God is not a liar, and He will keep His word.

But a little voice called worry steals in and reasons with you, saying, "Years ago you disobeyed the Lord financially, and now you will reap what you sowed." That may sound like a pretty good argument, and it may cause you to shift your meditation from God's Word to worry. Soon that little voice has grown so big it's like a megaphone in your ear. You forget that God said He would "keep him (or her) in perfect peace, whose mind is stayed on" Him (Isaiah 26:3).

ETERNAL LIFE POINT: Perfect peace means divine health, prosperity, wellness of being, and soundness of mind.

Stayed or *fixed* means "braced, lodged in an immovable position." But when we listen to worry, we become *unfixed*. Why does worry shout so loudly for our attention? Because if we look at it long enough, it will gain our trust. Pretty soon we begin praying out of fear, and eventually we quit praying and start looking for sympathy. We have trusted that other voice, and it won the affections of our heart.

Intentional Internal Focused Faith

Our personal relationship with Jesus Christ, through which fellowship (koinonia) is created with our Heavenly Father, establishes all other relationships.

ETERNAL LIFE POINT: Personal koinonia (fellowship) establishes intimacy with Christ Jesus that creates heavenly relationships that display Kingdom realities while here on earth.

God's purpose: To show that koinonia creates an intimacy with Christ Jesus that establishes a relationship that causes fellowship to flow to all who are related to God the Father

A little boy used to attend a church that had beautiful stained-glass windows picturing St. Matthew, St. Mark, St. Luke, St. John, St. Paul, and others. One day he was asked, "What is a saint?" He replied, "A saint is a person whom the light shines through." Not bad!

How many around us, these past few weeks, have seen the light shining through us? This question is not meant to be critical but is meant to challenge us to be sure that the presence of Christ Jesus is being heard and experienced as we the church are living out Kingdom life while in our world. We do know and realize that we the church are living saints in the world around us, right?

Today when people speak about a saint, invariably their concept of a saint is not the same as that's found in the Bible.

Roman Catholics understand a saint to be someone who is dead whose life conformed to church teaching and who has performed some miracles after dying, thereby qualifying them to be canonized and to become the object of prayer, devotion, and veneration (great respect).

However, the biblical teaching is quite different. The word *saint* means "one who is sanctified or set apart for God." It is not a statement of one's spiritual status that only a few Christians attain. On the contrary, a saint is anyone who has a living relationship with God through his mercy and grace expressed in the death of the Lord Jesus Christ. Hence, every Christian is a saint. They are seen and recognized as having fellowship (koinonia), an intimacy with Jesus Christ, as they live to share His love and grace with everyone who will receive the Good News. A good picture of how to identify a saint is found in these words:

Fellowship: a Reflection of One's Relationship to Christ Jesus

So by whatever [appeal to you there is in our mutual dwelling in Christ, by whatever] strengthening and consoling and encouraging [our relationship] in Him [affords], by whatever persuasive incentive there is in love, by whatever participation in the [Holy] Spirit [we share], and by whatever depth of affection and compassionate sympathy, fill up and complete my joy by living in harmony and being of the same mind and one in purpose, having the same love, being in full accord and of one harmonious mind and intention. Do nothing from factional motives [through contentiousness, strife, selfishness, or for unworthy ends] or prompted by conceit and empty arrogance. Instead, in the true spirit of humility (lowliness of mind) let each regard the others as better than and superior to himself [thinking more highly of one another than you do of yourselves]. Let each of you esteem and look upon and be concerned for not [merely] his own interests, but also each for the interests of others. (Philippians 2:1–4 AMPC)

ETERNAL LIFE POINT: A true follower of Jesus Christ truly takes on His identity. That's who we are as the saints of God, sons and daughters living in full harmony to fulfill the will of our Heavenly Father in all the earth.

Fellowship Begins with the Father and the Son "What we have seen and [ourselves] heard, we are also telling you, so that you too may realize and enjoy fellowship as partners and partakers with us. And [this]

fellowship that we have [which is a distinguishing mark of Christians] is with the Father and with His Son Jesus Christ (the Messiah)" (1 John 1:3 AMPC).

A Fellowship that Sacrifices
"Do not forget or neglect to do kindness and good, to be generous and distribute and contribute to the needy [of the church as embodiment and proof of fellowship], for such sacrifices are pleasing to God" (Hebrews 13:16 AMPC).

"So here's what I want you to do, God helping you: take your everyday, ordinary life—your sleeping, eating, going-to-work, and walking-around life—and place it before God as an offering. Embracing what God does for you is the best thing you can do for him. Don't become so well-adjusted to your culture that you fit into it without even thinking. Instead, fix your attention on God. You'll be changed from the inside out. Readily recognize what he wants from you, and quickly respond to it. Unlike the culture around you, always dragging you down to its level of immaturity, God brings the best out of you, develops well-formed maturity in you" (Romans 12:1–2 MSG).

The Fellowship of Acceptance
"If then you regard me a partner, accept him as you would me" (Philemon 1:17 NASB).

Key Marks of the Fellowship
"[So] if we say we are partakers together and enjoy fellowship with Him when we live and move and are walking about in darkness, we are [both] speaking falsely and do not live and practice the truth [which the Gospel presents]. But if we [really] are living and walking in the Light, as He [Himself] is in the Light, we have [true, unbroken] fellowship with one another, and the blood of Jesus Christ His Son cleanses (removes) us from all sin and guilt [keeps us cleansed from sin in all its forms and manifestations]" (1 John 1:6–7 AMPC).

Fellowship of Devotion
"And they steadfastly persevered, devoting themselves constantly to

the instruction and fellowship of the apostles, to the breaking of bread [including the Lord's Supper] and prayers" (Acts 2:42 AMPC).

ETERNAL LIFE POINT: Our true intentional internal focused faith creates true brotherhood. Our citizenship pertains to our relationship to Heaven, and of the "household of God" pertains to our relationship with God; whereas koinonia, the intimacy or fellowship with Christ Jesus, pertains and creates a family relationship of the saints to other believers. Before God, that relationship as brothers and sisters in Christ carries responsibilities to honor one another, build one another up, and function as one.

The fellowship (koinonia) of the saint is govern by an intimacy that is built and secured in the living expression "If I give everything I own to the poor and even go to the stake to be burned as a martyr, but I don't love, I've gotten nowhere. So, no matter what I say, what I believe, and what I do, I'm bankrupt without love. Love never gives up. Love cares more for others than for self. Love doesn't want what it doesn't have. Love doesn't strut, doesn't have a swelled head, doesn't force itself on others, isn't always 'me first,' doesn't fly off the handle, doesn't keep score of the sins of others, doesn't revel when others grovel, takes pleasure in the f lowering of truth, puts up with anything, trusts God always, always looks for the best, never looks back, but keeps going to the end" (1 Corinthians 13:3–7 MSG).

A New Living Way
"Therefore, brethren, since we have confidence to enter the holy place by the blood of Jesus, by a new and living way which He inaugurated for us through the veil, that is, His flesh, and since we have a great priest over the house of God, let us draw near with a sincere heart in full assurance of faith, having our hearts sprinkled clean from an evil conscience and our bodies washed with pure water. Let us hold fast the confession of our hope without wavering, for He who promised is faithful; and let us consider how to stimulate one another to love and good deeds, not forsaking our own assembling together, as is the habit

of some, but encouraging one another; and all the more as you see the day drawing near" (Hebrews 10:19–25 NASB).

Our intentional internal focused faith grows as we mature in our relationship with our Heavenly Father, through Jesus Christ, that creates a flow of endless love that establishes fellowship (koinonia) with our brothers and sisters through the fruit and empowerment of the Holy Spirit.

ETERNAL LIFE POINT: Love never dies! This is true fellowship; it always emulates the love of the Heavenly Father, Jesus Christ!

Concentrate and Meditate on These Words
Dear friends, listen well to my words. Keep my message in plain view at all times. Concentrate! Learn it by heart! Those who discover these words live, really live; body and soul, they're bursting with health. Keep vigilant watch over your heart; that's where life starts. (Proverbs 4:20–23 Message Bible)

God calls us friends; He has five commands:

1.   Listen well to His Words.
2.   Tune your ears to His voice.
3.   Keep His message in plain view at all times.
4.   Concentrate on it (intentional internal focused faith).
5.   Learn it by heart (memorize it).

Promise to be fulfilled for those who practice these Words: they will live, really live (abundantly), and their bodies and souls will be bursting with health.

1.   Write for yourself a life application.
2.   Memorize the scripture (intentional internal focused faith).
3.   Write a prayer from your life application to practice daily.
4.   Practice living the truth of your prayer daily.

Chapter 15

A FAMILY BEYOND DESCRIPTION

AND EMPOWERMENT!

Our Heavenly Father has never lost His heart for His family at the fall of man in the garden, for He had created man in His image and gave man His authority to subdue and rule all the earth.

When man gave away his authority to Satan, God let it be known that His authority would be taken back and given to His sons and daughters again.

"The Lord God said to the serpent, 'Because you have done this, cursed are you more than all cattle, and more than every beast of the field; on your belly you will go, and dust you will eat all the days of your life; and I will put enmity between you and the woman, and between your seed and her seed; he shall bruise you on the head, and you shall bruise him on the heel'" (Genesis 3:14–15 NASB).

The Fulfillment of This Prophecy

In Jesus Christ, you can belong to a family that's beyond description. This is not just in size but power as well. The family of God or the Body of Christ or the House of God all describe who we are together in Christ Jesus.

The Body of Christ Is Full of Himself (Christ Jesus) "Now there are varieties of gifts, but the same Spirit. And there are varieties of ministries, and the same Lord. There are varieties of effects, but the same God who works all things in all persons. But to each one is given the manifestation of the Spirit for the common good. For to one is given the word of wisdom through the Spirit, and to another the word of knowledge according to the same Spirit; to another faith by the same Spirit, and to another gifts of healing by the one Spirit, and to another the effecting of miracles, and to another prophecy, and to another the distinguishing of spirits, to another various kinds of tongues, and to another the interpretation of tongues. But one and the same Spirit works all these things, distributing to each one individually just as He wills. For even as the body is one and yet has many members, and all the members of the body, though they are many, are one body, so also is Christ. For by one Spirit we were all baptized into one body, whether Jews or Greeks, whether slaves or free, and we were all made to drink of one Spirit. For the body is not one member, but many" (1 Corinthians 12:4–14 NASB).

Our Eternal Function
The family of God, through her gifting by the Holy Spirit, is the continuation of the work of Christ Jesus on earth. The Body of Christ is the reflection of all the work Jesus displayed from Heaven to earth. The House of God is the unity of Christ's Body being fitted together for continuing to display the glory of Heaven on earth while continuing to destroy the works of Satan.

God's purpose: to show that whether we're known as the Body of Christ, the House of God, or the family of God, we are members in this world connected together without number and with resurrection empowerment to continue the work of Jesus Christ for destroying the works of Satan until all have heard and had an opportunity for receiving Jesus Christ and eternal life.

ETERNAL LIFE POINT: Father God wants His family back, and we, His body, are now commissioned and empowered to continue the work of our Savior and Lord Jesus Christ, declaring the good news and expanding Heaven's realities on earth.

God said to Satan, "And I will put enmity between you and the woman, and between your seed and her Seed; he shall bruise your head, and you shall bruise his heel" (Genesis 3:15).

When that prophecy was fulfilled in the death and resurrection of Jesus Christ, God took back the authority man had given away and reclaimed our purpose on this earth. He gave us a clear field to run toward the original goal—and run with all our might. We, the church, are called to extend His rule in this earthly sphere, just as Adam was called to do. We see this in each commission shown in the gospel: the commission of the twelve, the commission of the seventy and the seventy-two, and the Great Commission. God gave the same instructions to all who would be a part of His family: in essence, He said, "Go heal the sick, preach the good news, demonstrate who I am and what I am like. Extend My Kingdom!"

Three Mindsets Found in the Body of Christ Then and Now

The Leavens of the Mind
The Bible talks about influences on the mind that determine how we interact with the Kingdom. These influences affect us as we endeavor to become members of Christ's Body as well as how we think and act in the Body of Christ.

Jesus Teaching on the Leaven of the Mind
Jesus put it this way in Matthew 13:33 (another parable He spoke to them): "The kingdom of heaven is like leaven, which a woman took and hid in three measures of meal till it was all leavened."

Jesus spoke again of leaven in Mark 8:13–21:

And He left them, and getting into the boat again, departed to the other side. Now the disciples had forgotten to take bread, and they did not have more than one loaf with them in the boat. Then He charged them, saying, "Take heed, beware of the leaven of the Pharisees and the leaven of Herod." And they reasoned among themselves, saying, "It is because we have no bread." But Jesus, being aware of it, said to them, "Why do you reason because you have no bread? Do you not yet perceive nor understand? Is your heart still hardened? Having eyes, do you not see? And having ears, do you not hear? And do you not remember? When I broke the five loaves for the five thousand, how many baskets full of fragments did you take up?" They said to Him, "Twelve." "Also, when I broke the seven for the four thousand, how many large baskets full of fragments did you take up?" And they said, "Seven." So He said to them, "How is it you do not understand?

Our son David Paul enjoys making bread, so in his making of bread, he put some leaven and then put his dough next to some heat; the heat would mix with the leaven in the dough, causing it to rise.

This is a picture of us as believers and followers of Jesus Christ; the heat from the storms and struggles of life will cause the leaven of our minds to rise, revealing our true mindset (what we intentionally internally focus on).

Jesus's Warning

In saying, "Be careful of the leaven of the Pharisees and the leaven of Herod," He was warning them about influences on the mind that can rob us of the nutrients of revelation and renewal. Three kinds of leavens are mentioned in the above verses: the leaven of Herod, the Pharisees, and the Kingdom. These leavens are alive and active today, and they greatly affect how you think, how you live, and everything about your life.

1. The leaven of Herod is an atheistic influence based on the strength of man and man-based systems, like politics, popular

will, and persuasion. Herod's leaven excludes God entirely. Its statement of faith is cynical: "God helps those who help themselves."

2. The leaven of the Pharisees is different from Herod's. Pharisee leaven represents the religious system. It embraces God in theory but not in practice or experience. The concept of God is essential to the pharisaical mind, but the experience of God is completely removed. The Pharisees have God in form but without power.

3. Kingdom leaven thinking knows that anything is possible at any time. It's activated when you and I with tender hearts surrender to the thought patterns of God, when we receive His imaginations and say yes. We want our minds to be full of Kingdom leaven, Kingdom influence. We want miracles, and we want those miracles to have their full effect on us, changing the way we see and behave.

ETERNAL LIFE POINT: Our minds are the gateway to Heaven's realities, and the leaven that governs our process of bringing Heaven's realities is determined by what we are intentionally internally focused upon, the leaven of Herod, the leaven of the Pharisees, or the leaven of the Kingdom.

Not Many Followers

There are too few of us today who follow these precise instructions. We get caught up in side arguments, intellectual skirmishes, theories, and emotional head trips. We become enamored of our own talents and spiritual gifts, thinking we can direct our own course simply by putting our gifts and talents to use as we see fit.

Though well-intentioned, as many of us are, we become self-appointed in our commissions, honestly believing we are submitting to God. In reality, it isn't possible to prove the will of God on earth as it is in Heaven unless we are completely plugged into the primary mission God gave us (Romans 12:1–2).

It's Been Said This Way
"There is no CO-missioning without SUB-mission to the primary mission. So what is the primary mission?" (Bill Johnson, *The Supernatural Power of a Transformed Mind*).

We see it in the life of Jesus and in the testimony of scripture. First, John 3:8 states clearly that through intimacy with God, we are to destroy the works of the devil. "For this purpose the Son of God was manifested, that He might destroy the works of the devil" (1 John 3:8b).

That was Jesus's assignment, it was Adam and Eve's assignment, and it was the disciples' assignment. My brothers and sisters, this is our assignment as well. God's purpose in saving you and I was not simply to rescue us and let us keep busy until He shipped you and I off to Heaven. His purpose was much bigger, much more stunning. He commissioned you and I to demonstrate the will of God "on earth as it is in heaven," transforming this planet into a place radiant and saturated with His power and presence. This is the very backbone of the Great Commission, and it should define your life and my life in the family of God.

The Beginning of Identifying the Family
As Jesus was speaking to the crowd, his mother and brothers stood outside, asking to speak to him. Someone told Jesus, "Your mother and your brothers are standing outside, and they want to speak to you." Jesus asked, "Who is my mother? Who are my brothers?" Then he pointed to his disciples and said, "Look, these are my mother and brothers. Anyone who does the will of my Father in heaven is my brother and sister and mother!" (Matthew 12:46–50 NLT)

How does one truly become a part of the heavenly family? Jesus answered our question: "Jesus answered and said to them, 'This is the work of God, that you believe in Him whom He has sent'" (John 6:29 NASB).

"Anyone who does the will of my Father in Heaven!" Even before His death and resurrection, Jesus was declaring who would and how one would become a part of God's family.

ETERNAL LIFE POINT: The family of God is identified through the obedience of being heavenly minded, as every member in the Body is using their spiritual gifts to bring Heaven's realities to fulfill their Heavenly Father's will while on planet earth.

A Heavenly Minded Body Looks Like This

So, as those who have been chosen of God, holy and beloved, put on a heart of compassion, kindness, humility, gentleness and patience; bearing with one another, and forgiving each other, whoever has a complaint against anyone; just as the Lord forgave you, so also should you. Beyond all these things put on love, which is the perfect bond of unity. Let the peace of Christ rule in your hearts, to which indeed you were called in one body; and be thankful. Let the word of Christ richly dwell within you, with all wisdom teaching and admonishing one another with psalms and hymns and spiritual songs, singing with thankfulness in your hearts to God. Whatever you do in word or deed, do all in the name of the Lord Jesus, giving thanks through Him to God the Father. (Colossians 3:12–17 NASB)

A Heavenly Minded Body Is Govern by Love

Love is patient, love is kind and is not jealous; love does not brag and is not arrogant, does not act unbecomingly; it does not seek its own, is not provoked, does not take into account a wrong suffered, does not rejoice in unrighteousness, but rejoices with the truth; bears all things, believes all things, hopes all things, endures all things. (1 Corinthians 13:4–7 NASB)

Driven by the Commitment to Follow Christ

Example

For you have been called for this purpose, since Christ also suffered for you, leaving you an example for you to follow in His steps, WHO COMMITTED NO SIN, NOR WAS ANY DECEIT FOUND IN HIS MOUTH; and while being reviled, He did not revile in return; while suffering, He uttered no threats, but kept entrusting Himself to Him who judges righteously; and He Himself bore our sins in His body on the cross, so that we might die to sin and live to righteousness; for by His wounds you were healed. For you were continually straying like sheep, but now you have returned to the Shepherd and Guardian of your souls. (1 Peter 2:21–25 NASB)

Learning to Be a Heavenly Minded Family

Standing near the cross were Jesus' mother, and his mother's sister, Mary (the wife of Clopas), and Mary Magdalene. When Jesus saw his mother standing there beside the disciple he loved, he said to her, "Dear woman, here is your son." And he said to this disciple, "Here is your mother." And from then on this disciple took her into his home. (John 19:25–27 NLT)

Even when we lose our earthly father or mother or brother or sister, as believers and followers of Jesus Christ, we belong to a family that just keeps growing beyond comprehension and description.

We are children of God and a fellow heir with Christ. Before the foundation of the world, God had us in mind. He created us, and then He adopted us as His very own children. But it came at a price.

In order for us to be brought into God's family, His Son had to die. God gave His Son for us to be called sons. We know that Jesus's death wasn't short and quick. It was long and agonizing—and it was for us.

ETERNAL LIFE POINT: The only way to consistently do Kingdom works is to view and see Heaven's reality from God's perspective.

The Importance for Renewing Our Minds

This is what the Bible means when it talks about renewing our minds. The battle is in the mind. The mind is the essential tool in bringing Kingdom reality to the problems and crises people face.

God has made yours and my mind the gatekeeper of the supernatural. To be of any use to the Kingdom, our minds must be transformed. We find a clue to what that word means in the transfiguration of Jesus when He talked with Moses and Elijah. "And He was transfigured before them; and His face shone like the sun, and His garments became as white as light. And behold, Moses and Elijah appeared to them, talking with Him" (Matthew 17:2–3 NASB).

The reality of Heaven radiated through Jesus, and He shone with incredible brilliance. His body revealed the reality of another world. The word *transformed* in that passage is the same word we find in Romans 12:2. The *renewed mind* then reflects the reality of another world in the same way Jesus shone with Heaven's brilliance. "And do not be conformed to this world, but be transformed by the renewing of your mind, so that you may prove what the will of God is, that which is good and acceptable and perfect" (Romans 12:2 NASB).

It's not just that our thoughts are different but that our way of thinking is transformed because we think from a different reality—from Heaven toward earth! That is the transformed perspective. The renewed mind enables us, His co-laborers, to prove the will of God. We prove the will of God when we put on display the reality of Heaven.

The unrenewed mind, on the other hand, brings about a completely different manifestation: "Hear, O earth! Behold, I will certainly bring calamity on this people—the fruit of their thoughts, because they have not heeded My words nor My law, but rejected it" (Jeremiah 6:19).

The Family of God
The Father and Jesus have, from the beginning, planned to increase their kind. The God kind is a family! It is headed by the Father and now consists of the Father and the Son, Jesus Christ.

Ephesians 3:14–15 mentions "the Father of our Lord Jesus Christ, from whom the whole family in heaven and earth is named."

The Father and Christ existed from the beginning and always will exist. It is their plan and desire to add to their kind—"bringing many sons to glory" (Hebrews 2:10).

Just as all life was made to reproduce after its own kind as stated throughout Genesis 1, God patterned man after the God kind. This is the ultimate meaning of Genesis 1:26, where God says, "Let Us make man in Our image, according to Our likeness."

Conclusion
This is a two-stage process. First, God made man physical of the dust of the earth. Then through conversion and faith in Christ and obedience to God's spiritual law of love, each person becomes spiritually a "new creation" (2 Corinthians 5:17, Ephesians 4:24). This leads to the final birth of new children into the divine family, who are then like Christ Himself, the firstborn Son of God (Romans 8:29, Galatians 4:19, 1 John 3:2).

Indeed, just as human children are the same kind of beings as their parents (that is, human beings), so will God's children be the same kind of beings as the Father and Christ (that is, divine beings). This is the awesome destiny of mankind! The God family will expand through God's wonderful plan as revealed in His Word.

ETERNAL LIFE POINT: Therefore, the family of God is to continue the work of Jesus Christ, destroying the works of the enemy and bringing as many as we can into the heavenly family.

Concentrate and Meditate on These Words
Dear friends, listen well to my words. Keep my message in plain view at all times. Concentrate! Learn it by heart! Those who discover these words live, really live; body and soul, they're bursting with health. Keep vigilant watch over your heart; that's where life starts. (Proverbs 4:20–23 Message Bible)

God calls us friends; He has five commands:

1. Listen well to His Words.
2. Tune your ears to His voice.
3. Keep His message in plain view at all times.
4. Concentrate on it (intentional internal focused faith).
5. Learn it by heart (memorize it).

Promise to be fulfilled for those who practice these Words: they will live, really live (abundantly), and their bodies and souls will be bursting with health.

1. Write for yourself a life application.
2. Memorize the scripture (intentional internal focused faith).
3. Write a prayer from your life application to practice daily.
4. Practice living the truth of your prayer daily.

Chapter 16

ADOPTED TO A HIGHER STANDARD

God's purpose: to show that every believer, through the forethought of a loving Heavenly Father, was thought of before the foundation of the world. Our Father God was looking at redemption for everyone who would be born again and adopted through Jesus Christ as His very own children.

Do You Live Below Your Potential?

The average cost of adoption is one of the most difficult aspects of the adoption process for most families. Adoption, if you do not already know, can be expensive. It is a complicated legal process involving state and federal laws, as well as other important regulations. Completing an adoption requires an extensive amount of work, which can add up.

The average cost of adoption is dependent on several variables, like the type of adoption, the adoption professional, and other unique details of your situation. Each of these factors can influence typical adoption costs. Generally, for families adopting a baby through a private agency, the average cost of adoption in the US, according to a report from *Adoptive Families* magazine, is $43,000. While costs may vary on an individual basis, families typically spend in this range on the adoption process.

Variable Adoption Costs

These are typical adoption costs that can change based on each individual adoption situation. Variable costs are largely made up of expenses to support the prospective birth mother. These expenses are court-approved based on the adoption laws of the prospective birth mother's state. There are several types of variable expenses that could come up in an adoption:

1. *Legal.* The adoption process is guided by laws and regulations. There are piles of paperwork and potential court appearances involved, and an adoption attorney is necessary to navigate it all. The legal costs of the adoption, which can vary from case to case, are included in the typical adoption costs.
2. *Medical.* There are many medical expenses for the prospective birth mother and baby during the adoption process. In some cases, the bulk of these expenses can be covered by Medicaid or other insurance. However, the remainder of the bill falls into the variable adoption costs that can affect the average cost of adoption in the US.
3. *Living.* Living expenses help subsidize a prospective birth mother's financial needs during pregnancy, if necessary and allowed under state law. This type of adoption expense can vary significantly from case to case, but it is something that all hopeful adoptive parents will need to account for.

Variable adoption costs are the primary reason that most adoption agencies will quote adoptive families a range of average adoption costs rather than a hard number. There is room for flexibility here. However, it is uncommon for any of these expenses to skyrocket and cause the average cost of adoption to jump significantly from the initial estimate.

What Is the Average Cost to Adopt a Child with American Adoptions?

American adoptions' average cost of domestic adoption is in line with national averages. As we said above, *Adoptive Families* magazine found that the average price for adoption is $43,000. For our domestic adoption program, the average cost of adoption ranges from $40,000–$50,000.

What Your Adoption Costs

Why am I bringing adoption to the forefront? Because adoption is about who we are and what it cost our Heavenly Father to purchase us to be a part of His family.

Many people struggle with thoughts of adoption, let alone to think that they themselves have been adopted. Yet every believer's life is about being adopted. And because adoption is not in the forefront of our minds and hearts, we don't think or focus upon it as we really should. And it is here where we lose the understanding and potential of our true identity and our inheritance. If the church were to act on her true identity and inheritance, we would not be seeing all the conflict of people struggling for identity. We were created for relationships and to be identified as part of a family.

Great thought and measure have been taken for you so that you would always have an identity and share in your family's inheritance. Read these words and begin to reflect on your adoption; know how much you are loved:

Ephesians 1:3—"All praise to God, the Father of our Lord Jesus Christ, who has blessed us with every spiritual blessing in the heavenly realms because we are united with Christ."

Ephesians 1:4—"Even before he made the world, God loved us and chose us in Christ to be holy and without fault in his eyes."

Ephesians 1:5—"God decided in advance to adopt us into his own family by bringing us to himself through Jesus Christ. This is what he wanted to do, and it gave him great pleasure."

Ephesians 1:6—"So we praise God for the glorious grace he has poured out on us who belong to his dear Son."

Ephesians 1:7—"He is so rich in kindness and grace that he purchased our freedom with the blood of his Son and forgave our sins."

Ephesians 1:8—"He has showered his kindness on us, along with all wisdom and understanding."

Ephesians 1:9—"God has now revealed to us his mysterious plan regarding Christ, a plan to fulfill his own good pleasure."

Ephesians 1:10—"And this is the plan: at the right time he will bring everything together under the authority of Christ—everything in heaven and on earth."

Ephesians 1:11—"Furthermore, because we are united with Christ, we have received an inheritance from God, for he chose us in advance, and he makes everything work out according to his plan."

Ephesians 1:12—"God's purpose was that we Jews who were the first to trust in Christ would bring praise and glory to God."

Ephesians 1:13—"And now you Gentiles have also heard the truth, the Good News that God saves you. And when you believed in Christ, he identified you as his own by giving you the Holy Spirit, whom he promised long ago."

Ephesians 1:14—"The Spirit is God's guarantee that he will give us the inheritance he promised and that he has purchased us to be his own people. He did this so we would praise and glorify him."

There's more to come as we look at what it all cost God to adopt each one of us.

Be encouraged and unafraid, blessings!

The Adoption of Believers (Romans 8:15, 9:26; Galatians 3:26)

Romans 8:15—"For [the Spirit which] you have now received [is] not a spirit of slavery to put you once more in bondage to fear, but you have received the Spirit of adoption [the Spirit producing sonship] in [the bliss of] which we cry, abba (Father)! Father!"

Romans 9:26—"And it shall be that in the very place where it was said to them, you are not My people, they shall be called sons of the living God [Hosea 1:10]."

Galatians 3:26—"For in Christ Jesus you are all sons of God through faith."

ETERNAL LIFE POINT: Every believer's adoption is not a right but a privilege that creates their right as sons and daughters of a gracious and merciful Heavenly Father, Who adopted them into His eternal family.

One of the most interesting examples of adoption in history has to do with the emperor Claudius. Claudius adopted Nero to set up the political intrigue to allow Nero to succeed him as emperor of Rome. The two men were not, in any sense, blood relatives. Nero wished to cement the alliance by marrying Claudius's daughter, Octavia. Remember, Nero and Octave were in no sense blood relations; yet in the eyes of the law, they were brother and sister. Before they could marry, the Roman senate had to pass special legislation to allow the marriage to take place.

Our own adoption practices are patterned after the Roman laws.

Adoption in the Roman Law

Adoption was the legal action by which a person takes into his family a child not his own with the purpose of treating him as and giving him all the privileges of his own natural child. An adopted child was legally entitled to all rights and privileges of a natural-born child.

Colossians 1:13—"[The Father] has delivered and drawn us to Himself out of the control and the dominion of darkness and has transferred us into the kingdom of the Son of His love."

God has delivered us out of the authority of darkness and transferred us into the Kingdom of God, which is a realm of light (Colossians 1:13, Acts 26:18, 1 Peter 2:9).

Acts 26:18—"To open their eyes that they may turn from darkness to light and from the power of Satan to God, so that they may thus receive forgiveness and release from their sins and a place and portion among those who are consecrated and purified by faith in Me [Isaiah 42:7, 16]."

1 Peter 2:9—"But you are a chosen race, a royal priesthood, a dedicated nation, [God's] own purchased, special people, that you may set forth the wonderful deeds and display the virtues and perfections of Him Who called you out of darkness into His marvelous light [Exodus 19:5, 6]."

ETERNAL LIFE POINT: Every believer has been legally adopted from the kingdom and world of darkness into the Kingdom of life and light.

Roman Legal Practice

According to the Roman legal system, the person who was adopted into a family gained all the legal rights of a legitimate son in the new family, but he lost all the rights, privileges, and responsibilities in his old family. By becoming a member of the new family, he gained all the rights of his new father's estate. He was now an equal with the other sons and daughters in his new family. He was a coheir with them according to the law. He was regarded as a new person who had a new life in a new family.

Another wonderful thing about the Roman law was that the old life of the adopted son was completely wiped out. All his debts were cancelled. His past now had nothing to do with him. He was in a new relationship with a new family.

Jewish Life

In the Old Testament, God adopted the people of Israel as His own unique people. They enjoyed a special relationship as the chosen people of God. They were God's people by adoption (Romans 9:4, 26).

Romans 9:4—"For they are Israelites, and to them belong God's adoption [as a nation] and the glorious Presence (Shekinah). With them were the special covenants made, to them was the Law given. To them [the temple] worship was revealed and [God's own] promises announced [Exodus 4:22, Hosea 11:1]."

Romans 9:26—"And it shall be that in the very place where it was said to them, you are not My people, they shall be called sons of the living God [Hosea 1:10]."

Why did God choose Israel and not Babylon, Egypt, or Assyria? They were much larger and more powerful than Israel. Deuteronomy 7:6–8 tells us it was an act of God's grace. God told Moses, "For you are a holy people to the Lord your God; the Lord your God has chosen you to be a people for His own possession out of all the peoples who are on the face of the earth. The Lord did not set His love on you nor choose you because you were more in number than any of the peoples, for you were the fewest of all peoples, but because the Lord loved you and kept the oath which He swore to your forefathers, the Lord brought you out by a mighty hand and redeemed you from the house of slavery, from the hand of Pharaoh king of Egypt" (Deuteronomy 7:6–8).

God chose Israel as an act of love. Grace is written all over that choice. Moreover, the apostle Paul tells us the Holy Spirit is the witness to our adoption into the family of God. Have you ever wondered how you got into the family of God?

Christians' Privilege in the Family of God

Two things happened in our relationship to God's family the moment we believed on Christ as our Savior. The believing sinner, who is not a natural son or daughter of God, is positioned as an adult son in the family of God. This is a legal action and position. It is like a formal adoption or the legal placing of a child in a new family. Please keep in mind this is not the same as regeneration. It is the act of God that places the believer in His family as an adult son. At the same time, we are told in the scriptures the believer is spiritually born into the family of God. This is the new birth or regeneration. In this sense, we are as a child who needs to grow and develop. The believing sinner in his position is one of full privilege in the family of God; his practice, however, involves growth in grace and knowledge of Christ.

The believer is placed as an adult son in the family of God.

A believer under grace is placed as an adopted son in the family of God. When the apostle Paul speaks of our spiritual adoption by God, he uses the word *huiosthesia* (*huios*—a son; *thesis*—a placing) to place as a son. It is the place given to one to whom it does not belong. Galatians 3:26 says, "For you are all sons of God through faith in Christ Jesus." He is an adult son of God. It is used only in reference to a believer in this age of grace.

Adoption puts the emphasis on the position we have with God as His full-grown children. This spiritual adoption takes place at the time one is saved and thus becomes a child of God. The one thus placed has at once all the privilege and liberty of a full-grown person. Moreover, it also imposes on the believer the responsibilities of belonging to full maturity. Whatever God declares true of any believer, He addresses to all believers.

Because we have all been adopted, God expects all believers to behave accordingly. Every believer is indwelled by the Holy Spirit and has the same enabling. Our position as a full-grown child of God enables us to live the Christian life. There is no other way to live it. God doesn't just save us and turn us loose on the world. He saves us and indwells us with His presence and power so He can live His life through us.

When a lost sinner becomes a Christian, he enters into the very family of God. He does not deserve it. God—in His amazing love, grace, and mercy—has taken the lost, helpless, poverty-stricken, debt-laden sinner and adopted him into His own family so that the debts are canceled and the glory inherited. Jesus told Nicodemus, a Jewish religious leader, "Truly, truly, I say to you, unless one is born again, he cannot see the kingdom of God." There are no exceptions. We all must be born into the family of God.

The actual placement of the believer into the family of God is by this spiritual birth. This is the work of regeneration by the Holy Spirit. As a result of our spiritual birth, we become little children (*teknion*). The believer's relation to God as a child results from the new birth. "But as many as received Him, to them He gave the right to become children of God, even to those who believe in His name, who were born, not of blood nor of the will of the flesh nor of the will of man, but of God" (John 1:12–13). Because of this spiritual birth, we are to grow and become mature in our spiritual life.

What Does Adoption Teach Us?

God, in His mercy, has brought us into His absolute possession. The old life has no more rights over us; God has an absolute right to us. The past is canceled, and its debts are wiped out; we began a new life with God and become heirs of all His riches. Since that is true, we become joint heirs with Jesus Christ, God's unique son. That which Christ inherits, we also inherit. Since Christ was raised to life and glory, we also inherit that life and glory.

Conclusion
We are no longer members of Adam's family. We have a new father. We have a new head of the family. God the Father loves us and wants us to become members of His family. All our inheritance from Adam—with its sin and death—has been cancelled out, and we are now members

of another family. God is now our father, and Jesus is our big brother! What a privilege and honor to be members of His family.

Concentrate and Meditate on These Words
Dear friends, listen well to my words. Keep my message in plain view at all times. Concentrate! Learn it by heart! Those who discover these words live, really live; body and soul, they're bursting with health. Keep vigilant watch over your heart; that's where life starts. (Proverbs 4:20–23 Message Bible)

God calls us friends; He has five commands:

1. Listen well to His Words.
2. Tune your ears to His voice.
3. Keep His message in plain view at all times.
4. Concentrate on it (intentional internal focused faith).
5. Learn it by heart (memorize it).

Promise to be fulfilled for those who practice these Words: they will live, really live (abundantly), and their bodies and souls will be bursting with health.

1. Write for yourself a life application.
2. Memorize the scripture (intentional internal focused faith).
3. Write a prayer from your life application to practice daily.
4. Practice living the truth of your prayer daily.

Chapter 17

ADOPTED THROUGH THE BLOOD OF JESUS CHRIST

It all starts in the realm of the minds, with our ability to think and choose—the most powerful thing in the universe after God. If we are created in the image of God, with the ability to make choices that impact not only us but also everyone around us and the world we live in, what sense of responsibility and stewardship do you feel?

Do You Live Below Your Potential?

The average cost of adoption is one of the most difficult aspects of the adoption process for most families. Adoption, if you do not already know, can be expensive. It is a complicated legal process involving state and federal laws, as well as other important regulations. Completing an adoption requires an extensive amount of work, which can add up.

The average cost of adoption is dependent on several variables, like the type of adoption, the adoption professional and other unique details of your situation. Each of these factors can influence typical adoption costs. Generally, for families adopting a baby through a private agency, the average cost of adoption in the U.S., according to a report from adoptive Families Magazine, is $43,000. While costs may vary on an individual basis, families typically spend in this range on the adoption process.

Variable adoption Costs:

These are typical adoption costs that can change based on each individual adoption situation. Variable costs are largely made up of expenses to support the prospective birth mother. These expenses are court-approved based on the adoption laws of the prospective birth mother's state. There are several types of variable expenses that could come up in an adoption.

Legal: The adoption process is guided by laws and regulations. There are piles of paperwork and potential court appearances involved, and an adoption attorney is necessary to navigate it all. The legal costs of the adoption, which can vary from case to case, are included in the typical adoption costs.

Medical: There are many medical expenses for the prospective birth mother and baby during the adoption process. In some cases, the bulk of these expenses can be covered by Medicaid or other insurance. However, the remainder of the bill falls into the variable adoption costs that can affect the average cost of adoption in the U.S.

Living: Living expenses help subsidize a prospective birth mother's financial needs during pregnancy, if necessary and allowed under state law. This type of adoption expense can vary significantly from case to case, but it is something that all hopeful adoptive parents will need to account for.

Variable adoption costs are the primary reason that most adoption agencies will quote adoptive families a range of average adoption costs rather than a hard number. There is room for flexibility here. However, it is uncommon for any of these expenses to skyrocket and cause the average cost of adoption to jump significantly from the initial estimate.

What is the average Cost to adopt a Child with american adoptions?

American adoptions' average cost of domestic adoption is in line with national averages. As we said above, adoptive Families Magazine found that the average price for adoption is $43,000. For our domestic adoption program, the average cost of adoption ranges from $40,000–$50,000.

What's the Cost Of your adoption Cost?:

Why am I bringing adoption to the fore front? Because adoption is about who we are and what it cost our Heavenly Father to Purchase us to be a part of His family.

Many people struggle with thoughts of adoption, let alone to think that they themselves have been adopted. Yet, every believer's life is about being adopted, and because adoption is not in the fore front of our minds and hearts, we don't think or focus upon it as we really should. And it is here where we loose the understanding and potential of our true identity and our inheritance. If the Church were to act on Her true identity and use her rightful inheritance, we would not be seeing all the conflict of people struggling for identity and to belong. We were created for relationships and to be identified as part of God's family.

Great thought and measure have been taken for you; so that you would always have an identity and share in your family's inheritance. Read these words and begin to reflect on your adoption. Know how much you are loved.

Ephesians 1:3 all praise to God, the Father of our Lord Jesus Christ, who has blessed us with every spiritual blessing in the heavenly realms because we are united with Christ.

Ephesians 1:4 Even before He made the world, God loved us and chose us in Christ to be holy and without fault in His eyes.

Ephesians 1:5 God decided in advance to adopt us into His Own family by bringing us to Himself through Jesus Christ. This is what He wanted to do, and it gave Him great pleasure.

Ephesians 1:6 So we praise God for the glorious grace He has poured out on us who belong to His dear Son.

Ephesians 1:7 He is so rich in kindness and grace that He purchased our freedom with the blood of His Son and forgave our sins.

Ephesians 1:8 He has showered His kindness on us, along with all wisdom and understanding.

Ephesians 1:9 God has now revealed to us His mysterious plan regarding Christ, a plan to fulfill His Own good pleasure.

Ephesians 1:10 and this is the plan: at the right time He will bring everything together under the authority of Christ—everything in heaven and on earth.

The Blood Speaks a Better Word!

Ephesians 1:11 Furthermore, because we are united with Christ, we have received an inheritance from God, for He chose us in advance, and He makes everything work out according to His plan.

Ephesians 1:12 God's purpose was that we Jews who were the first to trust in Christ would bring praise and glory to God.

Ephesians 1:13 and now you Gentiles have also heard the truth, the Good News that God saves you. and when you believed in Christ, He identif ied you as His Own by giving you the Holy Spirit, whom He promised long ago.

Ephesians 1:14 the Spirit is God's guarantee that He will give us the inheritance He promised and that he has purchased us to be his own people. He did this so we would praise and glorify Him.

ETERNAL LIFE POINT: Every believer's adoption into the family of God, was the foreknowledge and the foresight before the foundation of the world. Our Heavenly Father purpose for every believer to be identif ied through Jesus Christ in their heirship and to share and function in and from their Heavenly inheritance.

The Holy Spirit's Empowerment To Sonship:

Romans 8:10 and Christ lives within you, so even though your body will die because of sin, the Spirit gives you life because you have been made right with God.

Romans 8:11 the Spirit of God, who raised Jesus from the dead, lives in you. And just as God raised Christ Jesus from the dead, He will give life to your mortal bodies by this same Spirit living within you.

Romans 8:12 therefore, dear brothers and sisters, you have no obligation to do what your sinful nature urges you to do.

Romans 8:13 For if you live by its dictates, you will die. But if through the power of the Spirit you put to death the deeds of your sinful nature, you will live.

Romans 8:14 For all who are led by the Spirit of God are children of God.

Romans 8:15 So you have not received a Spirit that makes you fearful slaves. instead, you received God's Spirit when He adopted you as His Own children. Now we call Him, "abba, Father."

Romans 8:16 For His Spirit joins with our spirit to affirm that we are God's children.

Romans 8:17 and since we are His children, we are His heirs. In fact, together with Christ we are heirs of God's glory. But if we are to share His glory, we must also share His suffering.

The Adoption of Believers Romans 8:15; 9:26; Galatians 3:26

Romans 8:15 For [the Spirit which] you have now received [is] not a spirit of slavery to put you once more in bondage to fear, but you have received the Spirit of adoption [the Spirit producing sonship] in [the bliss of] which we cry, abba (Father)! Father!

Romans 9:26 and it shall be that in the very place where it was said to them, you are not My people, they shall be called sons of the living God. [Hos. 1:10.]

Galatians 3:26 For in Christ Jesus you are all sons of God through faith. ETERNAL LIFE POINT: Every believer's adoption is not a right but a privilege that creates their right as sons and daughters of a gracious and merciful Heavenly Father, who adopted them into His Eternal family. History of adoption:

One of the most interesting examples of adoption in history has to do with the Emperor Claudius. Claudius adopted Nero to set up the political intrigue to allow Nero to succeed him as Emperor of rome. the two men were not in any sense blood relatives. Nero wished to cement the alliance by marring Claudius' daughter Octavia. Remember Nero and Octave were in no sense blood relations, yet, in the eyes of the law, they were brother and sister. Before they could marry, the roman senate had to pass special legislation to allow the marriage to take place.

Our own adoption practices are patterned after the roman laws.

ADOPTION IN THE ROMAN LAW

Adoption was the legal action by which a person takes into his family a child not his own with the purpose of treating him as and giving him all the privileges of his own natural child. An adopted child was legally entitled to all rights and privileges of a natural-born child.

Colossians 1:13 "[the Father] has delivered and drawn us to Himself out of the control and the dominion of darkness and has transferred us into the kingdom of the Son of His love..."

God has delivered us out of the authority of darkness and transferred us into the kingdom of God, which is a realm of light—Col. 1:13; acts 26:18; 1 Pet. 2:9:

Acts 26:18 To open their eyes that they may turn from darkness to light and from the power of Satan to God, so that they may thus receive forgiveness and release from their sins and a place and portion among those who are consecrated and purified by faith in Me. [Isa. 42:7, 16.]

1 Peter 2:9 But you are a chosen race, a royal priesthood, a dedicated nation, [God's] own purchased, special people, that you may set forth the wonderful deeds and display the virtues and perfections of Him Who called you out of darkness into His marvelous light. [Exod. 19:5, 6.]

ETERNAL LIFE POINT: Every believer has been legally adopted from the kingdom and world of darkness into the Kingdom of life and light.

Why God Chose Israel:
Deuteronomy 7:6-8 tells us it was an act of God's grace. God told Moses: "For you are a holy people to the Lord your God; the Lord your God has chosen you to be a people for His own possession out of all the peoples who are on the face of the earth. the Lord did not set His love on you nor choose you because you were more in number than any of the peoples, for you were the fewest of all peoples, but because the Lord loved you and kept the oath which He swore to your forefathers, the Lord brought you out by a mighty hand and redeemed you from the house of slavery, from the hand of Pharaoh king of Egypt" (Deuteronomy 7:6-8).

God chose Israel as an act of love. Grace is written all over that choice.

Moreover, the apostle Paul tells us the Holy Spirit is the witness to our adoption into the family of God.

CHRISTIAN'S PRIVILEGE IN THE FAMILY OF GOD

Two things happened in our relationship to God's family the moment we believed on Christ as our Savior. The believing sinner, who is not a natural son or daughter of God, is positioned as an adult son in the family of God. This is a legal action and position. It is like a formal adoption or the legal placing of a child in a new family. We must keep in mind this is not the same as regeneration. It is the act of God, which places the believer in His family as an adult son. At the same time we are told in the Scriptures the believer is spiritually born into the family of God. This is the new birth or regeneration. In this sense we are as a child who needs to grow and develop. The believing sinner in his position is one of full privilege in the family of God; his practice, however, involves growth in grace and knowledge of Christ.

The believer is placed as an adult son in the family of God.

A believer under grace is placed as an adopted son in the family of God. When the apostle Paul speaks of our spiritual adoption by God he uses the word *huiosthesia* (*huios* - a son) (*thesis* - a placing), to place as a son. It is the place given to one to whom it does not belong. Galatians 3:26 says, "For you are all sons of God through faith in Christ Jesus." He is an adult son of God. it is used only in reference to a believer in this age of grace.

Adoption put the emphasis on the position we have with God as His full–grown children. This spiritual adoption takes place at the time one is saved and thus becomes a child of God. The one thus placed has at once all the privilege and liberty of a full–grown person.

Moreover, it also imposes on the believer the responsibilities of belonging to full maturity. Whatever God declares true of any believer, He addresses to all believers.

Because we have all been adopted God expects all believers to behave accordingly. Every believer is indwelt by the Holy Spirit and has the same enabling. Our position as a full-grown child of God enables us to live the Christian life. There is no other way to live it. God doesn't just save us and turn us lose on the world. He saves us and indwells us with His presence and power so He can live His life through us.

When a lost sinner becomes a Christian he enters into the very family of God. He does not deserve it. God in His amazing love, grace and mercy has taken the lost, helpless, poverty-stricken, debt-laden sinner and adopted him into His own family, so that the debts are canceled and the glory inherited. Jesus told Nicodemus a Jewish religious leader, "truly, truly, I say to you, unless one is born again, he cannot see the kingdom of God." There are no exceptions. We all must be born into the family of God.

The actual placement of the believer into the family of God is by this spiritual birth. This is the work of regeneration by the Holy Spirit. As a result of our spiritual birth we become "little children" (*teknion*). The believer's relation to God as a child results from the new birth. "But as many as received Him, to them He gave the right to become children of God, even to those who believe in His name, who were born, not of blood nor of the will of the flesh nor of the will of man, but of God" (John 1:12, 13). Because of this spiritual birth we are to grow and become mature in our spiritual life.

What does adoption teach us?

God, in His mercy, has brought us into His absolute possession. The old life has no more rights over us; God has an absolute right to us. The past is canceled and its debts are wiped out; we began a new life with God and become heirs of all His riches. Since that is true, we become joint–heirs with Jesus Christ, God's unique Son. That which Christ inherits, we also inherit. Since Christ was raised to life and glory, we also inherit that life and glory.

CONCLUSiON:

We are no longer members of adam's family. We have a new father. We have a new head of the family. God the Father loves us and wants us to become members of His family. All of our inheritance from adam with its sin and death has been cancelled out and we are now members of another family. God is now our Father and Jesus is our big brother! What a privilege and honor to be members of His family.

Listen to these words as we begin to focus on our adoption by our Heavenly Father:

Ephesians 1:3—"All praise to God, the Father of our Lord Jesus Christ, who has blessed us with every spiritual blessing in the heavenly realms because we are united with Christ."

Ephesians 1:4—"Even before he made the world, God loved us and chose us in Christ to be holy and without fault in his eyes."

Ephesians 1:5—"God decided in advance to adopt us into his own family by bringing us to himself through Jesus Christ. This is what he wanted to do, and it gave him great pleasure."

1. Even before we were brought into the family of God, He had already decided to bless us with every spiritual blessing in the heavenly realms. That decision was made before we were concede.
2. Our Father God was loving us before the foundation of the world and had already chosen us to be in His family through Christ Jesus. He even planned on making us holy and without fault in His eyes.

How many of us would admit we have been living below our sonship and our inheritances?

Concentrate and Meditate on These Words
Dear friends, listen well to my words. Keep my message in plain view at all times. Concentrate! Learn it by heart! Those who discover these words live, really live; body and soul, they're bursting with health. Keep vigilant watch over your heart; that's where life starts. (Proverbs 4:20–23 Message Bible)

God calls us friends; He has five commands:

1. Listen well to His Words.
2. Tune your ears to His voice.
3. Keep His message in plain view at all times.
4. Concentrate on it (intentional internal focused faith).
5. Learn it by heart (memorize it).

Promise to be fulfilled for those who practice these Words: they will live, really live (abundantly), and their bodies and souls will be bursting with health.

1. Write for yourself a life application.
2. Memorize the scripture (intentional internal focused faith).
3. Write a prayer from your life application to practice daily.
4. Practice living the truth of your prayer daily.

Chapter 18

THE KINGDOM OF LIGHT BANISHES THE KINGDOM OF DARKNESS

Kingdom of God and Kingdom of Satan: Light versus Darkness

This is a teaching about two kingdoms. They are spiritual kingdoms. This does not mean they are imaginary or philosophical constructs. They are real but not political or geographical kingdoms. Rather, they are worldwide and exist in people's minds and hearts. Every person in the world belongs to one of these kingdoms.

ETERNAL LIFE POINT: Without the Kingdom of Light, there is no understanding, only intellectual knowledge and the elevation of pride and self-centeredness.

John 8:31—"So Jesus was saying to those Jews who had believed Him, 'If you continue in My word, then you are truly disciples of Mine.'"

John 8:32—"And you will know the truth, and the truth will make you free."

Freedom—isn't this what everyone is shouting and marching over?

God's purpose: To show that God rules by and through His own nature and darkness cannot and will not ever be a part or present in the Kingdom of Light.

ETERNAL LIFE POINT: Every true believer that has been born again and adopted into the Kingdom and family of God has been transferred into the full light of God so that they would receive the ability to see (spiritual insight) and understand (applied practicing of truth) while being the light in this darkened world.

"In the beginning God created the heavens and the earth. The earth was formless and empty, and darkness covered the deep waters. And the Spirit of God was hovering over the surface of the waters. Then God said, 'Let there be light,' and there was light" (Genesis 1:1–3 NLT).

"If the Good News we preach is hidden behind a veil, it is hidden only from people who are perishing. Satan, who is the god of this world, has blinded the minds of those who don't believe. They are unable to see the glorious light of the Good News. They don't understand this message about the glory of Christ, who is the exact likeness of God.

"For God, who said, 'Let there be light in the darkness,' has made this light shine in our hearts so we could know the glory of God that is seen in the face of Jesus Christ" (2 Corinthians 4:3–4, 6 NLT).

"In the beginning the Word already existed. The Word was with God, and the Word was God.

"The Word gave life to everything that was created, and his life brought light to everyone. The light shines in the darkness, and the darkness can never extinguish it" (John 1:1, 4–5 NLT). You know the truth, and the truth will set you free!

We process to consider a little further what the Kingdom of God is. We have seen that from the beginning there has been a great conflict in this universe as to WHO shall have the dominion. The New Testament speaks of two kingdoms—the Kingdom of God and the kingdom of Satan, the Kingdom of the Son of God's love and the kingdom of the one who wants to usurp the place of God's Son—and all through the history of this world, these two kingdoms have been in deadly conflict. As to the Kingdom of God, we have said it is the absolute sovereign rule of God. We speak of entering the Kingdom of God, and in that way, we think of the Kingdom of God as a sphere of God's rule, but there is something about that we must be very clear on, although it is not easy to explain.

ETERNAL LIFE POINT: God rules by His own nature! We often think of a kingdom being just a place and a number of people in that place, and then we think of some person—a dictator, an autocrat—having dominion in that place over those people.

God does not rule as an autocrat or as a dictator. God's Kingdom is composed of those like Himself. This is what it is going to be at the end. The Kingdom is coming now, and when it has fully come, it will just be, and only be, people who are like God Himself.

This is why each and every believer must have the promise of the infilling of the empowerment of the Holy Spirit, for the Holy Spirit brings the very nature of God into the lives of His adopted sons and daughters—the nature or fruit of love, joy, peace, patience, kindness, goodness, gentleness, faithfulness, and self-control.

Many do not understand what I mean when I say that God rules by His own nature. God's government is on the basis of what God is. This is how He is ruling now. When we say "Thy will be done," we have to go on immediately and say, "As in Heaven, so on earth."

ETERNAL LIFE POINT: The Kingdom of God is according to that which satisfies the nature of God.

We have, then, two things to consider. The first one is this: To belong to the Kingdom of God, we have to be reconstituted according to God.

Many do not understand that the door to the Kingdom is closed to every man and woman who has not been reconstituted according to God's nature. This is about yours and my born-again experience and, second, our adoption into the Kingdom and family of God.

Think of it like this: Someone wants to be in the Kingdom of God and they come to the door and on that door they see the word "Cannot." You cannot come in here. Something has to happen in you before you can come in here. This realm belongs to people who are altogether different from what you are by nature.

Jesus replied, "I tell you the truth, unless you are born again, you cannot see the Kingdom of God." "What do you mean?" exclaimed Nicodemus. "How can an old man go back into his mother's womb and be born again?" Jesus replied, "I assure you, no one can enter the Kingdom of God without being born of water and the Spirit. Humans can reproduce only human life, but the Holy Spirit gives birth to spiritual life. So don't be surprised when I say, 'You must be born again.' The wind blows wherever it wants. Just as you can hear the wind but can't tell where it comes from or where it is going, so you can't explain how people are born of the Spirit." "How are these things possible?" Nicodemus asked. Jesus replied, "You are a respected Jewish teacher, and yet you don't understand these things? I assure you, we tell you what we know and have seen, and yet you won't believe our testimony." (John 3:3–11 NLT)

ETERNAL LIFE POINT: If we are going to be in the Kingdom of God, something has got to happen that makes you and I suitable for that Kingdom.

Now we note that it was the Kingdom Nicodemus was concerned about. He was a very religious and highly educated man, a man held in high esteem among the men of this world. Perhaps you would have found no fault with him, but Jesus said to him, without any hesitation, "Except a man be born from above, he cannot 'SEE' the Kingdom of God" (John

3:3). Jesus even went on to say, "Except a man be born of water and the Spirit, he cannot 'ENTER' into the Kingdom of God" (John 3:5). Far from being able to ENTEr, he cannot even SEE.

There is something about this Kingdom of God that necessitates having an altogether new constitution. We are hearing a great deal in our time again about outer space, and we send men into it. Have you seen pictures of those men? You can hardly recognize that they are men! They are so laden with artificial apparatus that you can hardly see them. They have no natural qualification for living in outer space and have to have artificial lungs. In a sense, they have to be reconstituted upon another principle. Jesus was saying to Nicodemus, "Nicodemus, if you got into the Kingdom of God you would die, you have not the equipment to live in this rare atmosphere."

ETERNAL LIFE POINT: For a nonbeliever to enter the Kingdom of God, he or she must have the right garments; for without, they would die. They are not constituted according to the realm of God.

ETERNAL LIFE POINT: Every true son and daughter of God, through their new birth experience, enters the Kingdom of God and receives the outer garment of adoption that equips them to operate from the spiritual light of understanding.

The Kingdom of God is everything that God is in His own nature. It is not just a sphere in which God rules as an autocrat. It is a realm in which God's nature is expressed.

Apostle Peter gives us a picture of the garment: "And because of his glory and excellence, he has given us great and precious promises. These are the promises that enable you to share his divine nature and escape the world's corruption caused by human desires" (2 Peter 1:4 NLT).

ETERNAL LIFE POINT: The Kingdom of God is ruled by and through divine light!

The scripture says, "God is light, and in Him is no darkness at all" (1

John 1:5), so the Kingdom of God is the rule of divine light, but divine light has always been a focal point of intense conflict.

The Bible opens with a conflict. There was a state of things in nature that God attacks—He begins to make a tremendous assault upon a condition of things, and the first attack of God was upon darkness. "Darkness was upon the face of the deep."

Light and darkness have been battling through the whole Bible; we read of it from the Old Testament all the way throughout the New Testament. There is a tremendous conflict between the Kingdom of Light and the kingdom of darkness.

If Satan can keep you in darkness, then he can keep you from *seeing* and *understanding*; he can keep you from receiving your inheritance.
Our born-again experience and our adoption garments must be put on in order for each one of us to be able to *see* and *understand*.

In 1 Corinthians 4:4, we are brought right to the very work of the devil: "The god of this world has blinded." The supreme work of Satan is to blind men and women from the light of truth.

The Life and Light

"He existed in the beginning with God. God created everything through him, and nothing was created except through him. The Word gave life to everything that was created, and his life brought light to everyone. The light shines in the darkness, and the darkness can never extinguish it" (John 1:2–5 NLT).

It is not that Satan makes good men bad or that he drags good men down into the mire of sin or that he brings strong young men and women down into moral corruption or makes atheists and infidels. These are only by-products; they are the result of something else, and that is this: "The god of this world has BLINDED our mind from SEEING AND UNDERSTANDING the Light of truth."

ETERNAL LIFE POINT: The work of the devil is to keep people in the dark!

Light is the most fatal thing to the kingdom of Satan; he fears light more than anything else. He has blinded the minds of the unbelieving, and why has he done so? It's a precaution against something, and one little word explains it: "Lest the Light of the gospel of the glory of Christ should shine." Satan loses power and authority over every believer who puts on the garment of understanding, and the garment of understanding comes from the ability to see spiritual truth about oneself from the light of revelation, Jesus Christ.

The Lord said, "You are the light of the World" (Matthew 5:14). Here is our challenge.

ETERNAL LIFE POINT: Divine light is positive. You cannot have divine light and be neutral.

Conclusion
"He who believes in Him is not judged; he who does not believe has been judged already, because he has not believed in the name of the only begotten Son of God. This is the judgment, that the Light has come into the world, and men loved the darkness rather than the Light, for their deeds were evil. For everyone who does evil hates the Light, and does not come to the Light for fear that his deeds will be exposed. But he who practices the truth comes to the Light, so that his deeds may be manifested as having been wrought in God" (John 3:18–21 NASB).

"But he who practices truth [who does what is right] comes out into the Light; so that his works may be plainly shown to be what they are—wrought with God [divinely prompted, done with God's help, in dependence upon Him]" (John 3:21 AMPC).

Romans 8:16—"For His Spirit joins with our spirit to affirm that we are God's children."

Romans 8:17—"And since we are His children, we are His heirs. In fact, together with Christ we are heirs of God's glory. But if we are to share His glory, we must also share His suffering."

Our born-again experience is the inner garment that we each put on to enter the Kingdom and family of God, and our adoption is our outer garment and status of our inherence to display the shining light of our understanding of the glorious gospel of Jesus Christ.

Our spiritual ability to see and understand exposes the darkness of Satan, and because we know the truth, we are free to live as the true sons and daughters of God.

An Exercise for Spiritual Seeing and Understanding

The Two Spiritual Kingdoms

There are certain things that need to be considered in every kingdom:

- First, there needs to be a *monarch*. So every kingdom is concerned with having someone crowned and enthroned as ruler.
- Next, every kingdom has to have a *realm* or territory over which its monarch rules.
- That realm must be occupied by *citizens*.
- The citizens must abide by certain *laws* issued by the monarch.
- The citizens must also live by certain distinguishing *customs*.
- A kingdom is concerned with its strength and *power* in conquering and defending.
- A kingdom is also concerned with its *destiny*—whether it will fall to ruin or rise to glory.

The seven considerations are true of spiritual kingdoms too. They are true of Christ's Kingdom, and they are true of Satan's.

Questions You Must Ask Yourself

To help you make a personal application of the study, here are some questions to consider:

- Am I acknowledging Jesus as my Lord and King, or am I by default letting Satan have dominion over me?
- Though Christ's Kingdom is in the world where I am, it is the Kingdom of Heaven and not of the world. So where is my life and heart centered? Are my affections for this world or for the heavenly realms?
- Am I a true believer in Jesus Christ and therefore a citizen of His Kingdom, or am I an unbeliever and therefore an alien to His realm?
- Do I keep the commands of Jesus, both believing and obeying the gospel, or am I a lawless one deceived into disregard of His covenant law?
- Is it my custom and habit to show the light and spirit of Christ in my daily conduct, or am I walking in darkness and fleshly lusts?
- Am I living in the power and victory of Jesus, more than a conqueror through Him (Romans 8:37), or am I living in my own weakness and failure under the illusion that I am strong?
- What is my destiny? I can ask no question more important than this. My destiny cannot be something in this life because the last thing that will happen to me in this life is my death. Have I secured life after death, eternal life in heavenly glory with Christ? Or is He going to send me away into everlasting punishment because I did not honor Him as my King and become a loyal citizen of His Kingdom under His blessing?

Pray a prayer that acknowledges your spiritual sight and understanding based off these questions.

Concentrate and Meditate on These Words
Dear friends, listen well to my words. Keep my message in plain view at all times. Concentrate! Learn it by heart! Those who discover these words live, really live; body and soul, they're bursting with health. Keep vigilant watch over your heart; that's where life starts. (Proverbs 4:20–23 Message Bible)

God calls us friends; He has five commands:

1. Listen well to His Words.
2. Tune your ears to His voice.
3. Keep His message in plain view at all times.
4. Concentrate on it (intentional internal focused faith)).
5. Learn it by heart (memorize it).

Promise to be fulfilled for those who practice these Words: They will live, really live (abundantly), and their bodies and souls will be bursting with health.

1. Write for yourself a life application.
2. Memorize the scripture (intentional internal focused faith).
3. Write a prayer from your life application to practice daily.
4. Practice living the truth of your prayer daily.

Chapter 19

LIVING LIFE FROM A NEW KINGDOM

Have you ever stopped and begin to consider why you say or do the things you are saying and doing? How much of who we are reflects the kingdom of which we are a part of? Our thoughts, spoken words, and actions are the reflection of the kingdom we have chosen to walk from each day.

"But I say, walk by the Spirit, and you will not carry out the desire of the flesh. For the flesh sets its desire against the Spirit, and the Spirit against the flesh; for these are in opposition to one another, so that you may not do the things that you please. But if you are led by the Spirit, you are not under the Law" (Galatians 5:16–18 NASB).

ETERNAL LIFE POINT: Being led by the Spirit is a choice of submitting and surrendering to the work of Christ Jesus in and over your daily life.

God's Purpose: to show that every believer has been given the divine nature and empowerment to live from Heaven to earth as the sons and daughters of their Heavenly Father.

Salt and Light

What does it look like living life from the Kingdom of God as His sons and daughters while still on earth? The church is the colony of Heaven placed on earth to be salt and light to a fallen world. The church is to give expression of the nature of God, drawing humanity to the mercy and grace of a loving, forgiving Heavenly Father. Our Heavenly Father desires no man to perish but that each would spend all eternity with Him.

Declaration and Directive

Matthew 5:13—"You are the salt of the earth; but if the salt has become tasteless, how can it be made salty again? It is no longer good for anything, except to be thrown out and trampled underfoot by men."

Matthew 5:14—"You are the light of the world. A city set on a hill cannot be hidden."

Matthew 5:15—"Nor does anyone light a lamp and put it under a basket, but on the lampstand, and it gives light to all who are in the house."

Matthew 5:16—"Let your light shine before men in such a way that they may see your good works, and glorify your Father who is in heaven."

Living Life from the New Kingdom

Over the next few minutes, I will share the Father's heart for the church and her life-giving expressions that declare that we the church are living from Heaven to earth.

This teaching is about living life from the kingdom while here on planet earth. We have been transferred from a spiritual kingdom of darkness to a spiritual kingdom of life and light. This does not mean they are imaginary or philosophical constructs. They are real but not political or geographical kingdoms. Rather, they are worldwide and exist in people's minds and hearts. Every person in the world belongs to one of these kingdoms.

Entering the Kingdom of Light
First Step
Jesus replied, "I tell you the truth, unless you are born again, you cannot see the Kingdom of God." "What do you mean?" exclaimed Nicodemus. "How can an old man go back into his mother's womb and be born again?" Jesus replied, "I assure you, no one can enter the Kingdom of God without being born of water and the Spirit. Humans can reproduce only human life, but the Holy Spirit gives birth to spiritual life. So don't be surprised when I say, 'You must be born again.' The wind blows wherever it wants. Just as you can hear the wind but can't tell where it comes from or where it is going, so you can't explain how people are born of the Spirit." "How are these things possible?" Nicodemus asked. Jesus replied, "You are a respected Jewish teacher, and yet you don't understand these things? I assure you, we tell you what we know and have seen, and yet you won't believe our testimony." (John 3:3–11 NLT)

ETERNAL LIFE POINT: The Kingdom of God is according to that which satisfies the nature of God.

ETERNAL LIFE POINT: If we are going to be in the Kingdom of God, something has got to happen that makes you and I suitable for that Kingdom.

These two life points are upmost in being able to enter the Kingdom of God as a son or daughter.

"Except a man be born from above, he cannot 'SEE' the Kingdom of God" (John 3:3).

Jesus even went on to say, "Except a man be born of water and the Spirit, he cannot 'ENTER' into the Kingdom of God" (John 3:5). Far from being able to ENTER, he cannot even SEE.

There is something about this Kingdom of God that necessitates having an altogether new constitution.

We are hearing a great deal in our time again about outer space, and we send men into it. Have you seen pictures of those men? You can hardly recognize that they are men!

They are so laden with artif icial apparatus that you can hardly see them. They have no natural qualification for living in outer space, and have to have artif icial lungs.

In a sense, they have to be reconstituted upon another principle. Jesus was saying to Nicodemus: "Nicodemus, if you got into the Kingdom of God you would die, you have not the equipment to live in this rare atmosphere."

ETERNAL LIFE POINT: For a non believer to enter the Kingdom of God he or she must have the right garments, for without, they would die. They are not constituted according to the realm of God.

ETERNAL LIFE POINT: Every true son and daughter of God, through their New Birth experience, enter the Kingdom of God and receives the outer garment of adoption, that equip them to operate from the spiritual light of understanding.

The Kingdom of God is everything that God is in His Own nature. It is not just a sphere in which God rules as an autocrat. It is a realm in which God's nature is expressed.

Our born-again experience constitutes brings us to our adoption as sons and daughters that equips us to begin to live from Heaven to earth. We must stop here before we can go any farther, making sure we are properly equipped for living Heaven's reality on earth. We must invite Jesus Christ into our lives in order for us to carry out our calling and purpose from Heaven to earth.

Pray This Prayer

Father God, I thank You for Jesus, Your Son, dying for me on the cross and for all my sins. I now confess that I am a sinner and invite Jesus Christ into my life, asking for forgiveness. I ask that He would sit on the throne of my heart to lead me into Kingdom living. Thank You for forgiving me of all my sins! In Jesus name I ask this!

With this exercise, we have just taken the first step to Kingdom living on earth. Now we'll begin to consider the mind and heart attitudes for fulfilling our call and purpose of Heaven's reality while on planet earth.

Our garments of our new birth and our adoption as sons and daughters are a must to enter the Kingdom of God and to receive our inheritance with the ability to see and to understand how to live a spiritual life from Heaven to earth.

Two Requirements of Belief

1. The requirement of the new birth and our adoption is one element of being able to function from Heaven to earth.
2. Every believer must be filled with the empowerment of the Holy Spirit.

Less one is born of the Spirit, there can be no spiritual natural revelation and understanding. The Holy Spirit will lead and teach us all truth.

John 14:26—"But the Helper, the Holy Spirit, whom the Father will send in My name, He will teach you all things, and bring to your remembrance all that I said to you."

Acts 1:8—"But you will receive power when the Holy Spirit has come upon you; and you shall be My witnesses both in Jerusalem, and in all Judea and Samaria, and even to the remotest part of the earth."

The Holy Spirit Establishes Our First Mind Living from Heaven to earth starts with having the same attitude as Christ Jesus.

Philippians 2:5–7—"Have this attitude in yourselves which was also in Christ Jesus, who, although He existed in the form of God, did not regard equality with God a thing to be grasped, but emptied Himself, taking the form of a bond-servant, and being made in the likeness of men."

Without this mindset, there is no spiritual enlightenment or spiritual understanding. We are left on our own trying to figure out the mind and heart of God while void of any empowerment. This seem to be a battle for many believers to fully understand and to accept. This is not about our physical ability and intellect; it's about our faith in the Word of God that takes us above our earthly understanding to a spiritual understanding that comes right from the mind and heart of God Himself.

"For to us God revealed them through the Spirit; for the Spirit searches all things, even the depths of God . . . Now we have received, not the spirit of the world, but the Spirit who is from God, so that we may know the things freely given to us by God" (1 Corinthians 2:10, 12 NASB).

The Battle Within the Mind and Heart
This is every believer's battle: The emptying of oneself for the sake of Christ Jesus in behalf of others. This is a requirement for living from Heaven to earth. To do nothing from your own initiative is the battle of the flesh versus the spirit. Our attitudes must be taking the form of a bond servant and being made in the likeness of our Lord Jesus Christ. It is only as we practice this mind and heart attitude that we'll fulfill the scripture that says these:

Philippians 2—"Be Like Christ"

Philippians 2:1–4—"Therefore if there is any encouragement in Christ, if there is any consolation of love, if there is any fellowship of the Spirit, if any affection and compassion, make my joy complete by being of the same mind, maintaining the same love, united in spirit, intent on one purpose. Do nothing from selfishness or empty conceit, but with humility of mind regard one another as more important than yourselves; do not merely look out for your own personal interests, but also for the interests of others."

This mindset is a prerequisite of living from Heaven to earth, and it only happens through our spiritual birth and adoption as sons and daughters into the Kingdom and family of God.

This should be our first predetermined mind and heart attitude each morning as we endeavor to bring Heaven's realities into this darken world around us.

Thankful for My Freedom in Christ

1 Corinthians 6:12—"All things are lawful for me, but not all things are profitable. All things are lawful for me, but I will not be mastered by anything."

Although the apostle Paul speaks this verse in context to food, the principle of the verse can be applied not only in what one eats.

1 Corinthians 9:19—"For though I am free from all men, I have made myself a slave to all, so that I may win more."

The apostle Paul also said it like this: "All things are lawful, but not all things are profitable. All things are lawful, but not all things edify" (1 Corinthians 10:23).

Though we are free in Christ Jesus, the truth we need to be fully aware of "is that of something or someone mastering us and the principle of what is profitable or edifying."

And what is the key to all this as we live from Heaven to earth? We begin to establish our heavenly mindset. Today, we must consider this also as part of our daily mind and heart attitude.

Second Mindset: On the Things Above
Therefore if you have been raised up with Christ, keep seeking the

things above, where Christ is, seated at the right hand of God. Set your mind on the things above, not on the things that are on earth. For you have died and your life is hidden with Christ in God. When Christ, who is our life, is revealed, then you also will be revealed with Him in glory. (Colossians 3:1–4 NASB)

ETERNAL LIFE POINT: Our Heavenly Father intense that every one of His sons and daughters are to live from Heaven to earth.

As a young man longing to follow Jesus with all my heart and live as He wanted me to, I was told—and I am sure this person was trying to be encouraging when they declare these words—"David, you cannot be so heavenly minded that you do no earthly good." Sounds great if you're a person who thinks from earth to Heaven. It's this kind of thinking and attitude though that causes believers today to wish that God would heal, deliver, and bring more of Himself into our lives. And then we settle for "This must not be God's will for me. This troubling ordeal is my thorn in the flesh, like the apostle Paul." It's interesting how we take what's troubling others and make them our cross to carry.

Scripture encourages to set our minds on the thing above, not on the things of the earth. Why, because as a born-again believer and the adopted son or daughter of God, it's my inherited nature of my Heavenly Father that is on display; I am now created in the likeness of my elderly brother, Jesus Christ.

ETERNAL LIFE POINT: If Christ Jesus is going to have and give expression from Heaven to earth today, it's because you choose the mindset and heart attitude to let Him live in your place today.

This cannot be a once-in-a-while mindset and heart attitude; this must be practiced on a daily basis. We are Heaven's reality to be expressed while here on planet earth.

Living Life from the New Kingdom
This is one of scripture's greatest examples of living from Heaven to earth discretions that encourage each believer to practice their

heavenly mandate. Read it slowly and focus on what we as believers are admonished to do through the divine empowerment that has been granted to us as copartners in the divine nature of Jesus Christ.

Walking with Heaven's Empowerment

By his divine power, God has given us everything we need for living a godly life. We have received all of this by coming to know Him, the one who called us to Himself by means of His marvelous glory and excellence. And because of His glory and excellence, He has given us great and precious promises. These are the promises that enable you to share His Divine Nature and escape the world's corruption caused by human desires. In view of all this, make every effort to respond to God's promises. Supplement your faith with a generous provision of moral excellence, and moral excellence with knowledge, and knowledge with self-control, and self-control with patient endurance, and patient endurance with godliness, and godliness with brotherly affection, and brotherly affection with love for everyone. The more you grow like this, the more productive and useful you will be in your knowledge of our Lord Jesus Christ. But those who fail to develop in this way are shortsighted or blind, forgetting that they have been cleansed from their old sins. So, dear brothers and sisters, work hard to prove that you really are among those God has called and chosen. Do these things, and you will never fall away. Then God will give you a grand entrance into the eternal Kingdom of our Lord and Savior Jesus Christ. (2 Peter 1:3–11 NLT)

ETERNAL LIFE POINT: The divine nature of Jesus Christ is expressed through the empowerment of the Holy Spirit that we exercise daily in our diligence of practice faith, declaring with our lived life the character traits of our Heavenly Father Whose fruit renders us productive and useful for Kingdom living on planet earth.

This is truly a divine admonition for each and every believer. They need to have intentional internal focused faith for their daily mind and heart attitude for living Heaven's realities before the world around them. This is not something that just happens because we wish it so. There must be intentional internal focus that truly allows Jesus Christ to live in our place.

"Your old life is dead. Your new life, which is your real life—even though invisible to spectators—is with Christ in God. He is your life. When Christ (your real life, remember) shows up again on this earth, you'll show up, too—the real you, the glorious you. Meanwhile, be content with obscurity, like Christ" (Colossians 3:3–4 MSG).

ETERNAL LIFE POINT: The believers' obscurity to self is the only means and way that will allow Christ Jesus to have expression on earth today.

Why is it so important to live from Heaven to earth? Our answer is found in the last mindset and heart attitude that we must give daily expression to.

Conclusion
The Mindset of All Mindsets
Here is the most difficult mind and heart attitude to grow into and can only happen through a daily intentional internal focused faith. We have learned that we are copartners in the divine power and nature of God so that we may escape the world's corruption caused by human desires. Learning to lay our lives down for the sake of Christ Jesus in behalf of others is the most difficult battle in believers' life, especially when we don't feel that they deserve it. Has there ever been a time when any of us deserved God's grace and mercy? But He loved us anyway, and now we are Kingdom's reality and expression even to those we feel don't deserve it. This is why we don't live by the emotional dictate of our flesh but by the mindset of the Spirit. The mindset of the Spirit is life and peace. The mindset of the flesh is death and spiritual separation from God. The choice is yours!

ETERNAL LIFE POINT: Every believer in Jesus Christ is called and purposed to follow the example of the Lord Jesus Christ, Who is their real life while on planet earth. No exceptions!

"For you have been called for this purpose, since Christ also suffered for you, leaving you an example for you to follow in His steps, WHO COMMITTED NO SIN, NOR WAS ANY DECEIT FOUND IN HIS MOUTH; and while being reviled, He did not revile in return; while suffering, He uttered no threats, but kept entrusting Himself to Him who judges righteously; and He Himself bore our sins in His body on the cross, so that we might die to sin and live to righteousness; for by His wounds you were healed. For you were continually straying like sheep, but now you have returned to the Shepherd and Guardian of your souls" (1 Peter 2:21–25 NASB).

This is what living life from the New Kingdom looks like! We are to look, sound, and act like our Lord Jesus Christ, Who is our real life. This must be our intentional internal focused faith each and every morning of awaking. We must see it, and we must understand it when all darkness is pushing in on us!

"For we are His workmanship, created in Christ Jesus for good works, which God prepared beforehand so that we would walk in them" (Ephesians 2:10 NASB).

ETERNAL LIFE POINT: Walking by faith with the mindset of the Spirit is a choice over walking by the mindset of the flesh. It's our choice of the Spirit's mindset that gives expression to Heaven's realities while serving the Kingdom of God on earth.

Concentrate and Meditate on These Words
Dear friends, listen well to my words. Keep my message in plain view at all times. Concentrate! Learn it by heart! Those who discover these words live, really live; body and soul, they're bursting with health. Keep vigilant watch over your heart; that's where life starts. (Proverbs 4:20–23 Message Bible)

God calls us friends; He has five commands:

1. Listen well to His Words.
2. Tune your ears to His voice.

3. Keep His message in plain view at all times.
4. Concentrate on it (intentional internal focused faith).
5. Learn it by heart (memorize it).

Promise to be fulfilled for those who practice these Words: they will live, really live (abundantly), and their bodies and souls will be bursting with health.

1. Write for yourself a life application.
2. Memorize the scripture (intentional internal focused faith).
3. Write a prayer from your life application to practice daily.
4. Practice living the truth of your prayer daily.